Corporate Sponsorship in 3 Easy Steps

"Linda Hollander is amazing with the amount of knowledge and information she has about sponsorships and her ability to communicate it to those of us who are not familiar with the industry. I can now go out and get top-tier sponsors and she has turned my dreams into reality. I would encourage anyone interested in sponsorships to check her out. She is awesome!"

— **Jason Moss, Georgia Manufacturing Expo**

"I've worked with Linda Hollander for several years and she really knows what she's talking about. She has personally guided me and my team to getting a quick "yes," and we got a $100,000 sponsorship. I highly recommend *Corporate Sponsorship in 3 Easy Steps* if you want funding from sponsors."

— **Bryan Caplovitz, SpeakerMatch**

"Linda Hollander's expertise is phenomenal. In the world of sponsorships, don't get started without her help."

— **Ward Luthi, Author, Speaker and Adventure Traveler**

"Linda Hollander helped me get over $175,000 in sponsorships for my charity that brings clean water to people in need."

— **Amanda Mineer, Give Clean Water**

"Linda Hollander is a role model for business success and how to gain corporate sponsorships. While her life story inspires, it's her ability to guide others to build the business of their dreams that continues to get rave results. I highly recommend *Corporate Sponsorship in 3 Easy Steps* if you are serious about getting funding from corporate sponsors."

— **Anastasia Montejano, Visionary Leaders Breakthrough Program**

"Because of the information I got from Linda Hollander, I was able to bring in an additional $15,000 in conference sponsorships!"

— **Christopher Holliday, Ph.D., MPH, Business Owner and Event Producer**

"Rule #1 in sales is to under-promise and over-deliver. That is exactly what Linda Hollander does. When the student is ready the teacher appears – I was ready to learn when *Corporate Sponsorship in 3 Easy Steps* became available – that was no coincidence. I would recommend this book to anyone serious about attracting corporate sponsors."

— **Barbara J. Bruno, CPC, CTS, Career Coach and Recruiter**

"Linda Hollander is a 'Godsend!' I do not use that word lightly and can't recall using it to describe an author in the past. But, with the amount of information she shares, the word is perfect for her. If you want to get sponsors, you need to run (not walk) to get her sponsor training. Few people have

"Anyone who reads this book can quickly go from feeling dumb and ignorant to being bold and confident about obtaining sponsors."

— **Clive Swersky, Television Host and Producer**

"Stop worrying about how you're going to get clients to pay your bills. Live a bigger life. *Corporate Sponsorship in 3 Easy Steps* can change your whole approach to small business, and Linda Hollander's knowledge, honesty and exuberant personality make it a joy!"

— **Mary Lyn Miller, Speaker, Author and Business Owner**

"When we started working with Linda Hollander, money was really tight. Pretty soon she was reaching out to some of the biggest companies in America for sponsorships and people started saying "yes" to us. Now companies are sponsoring us with really large sums of money and we're a pretty new business. I strongly recommend Linda Hollander. Her knowledge about sponsors is phenomenal."

— **Harlan Kilstein, Business Owner**

"Linda Hollander is an absolute genius and wholeheartedly generous. The information and support I have received from her is invaluable and will serve to open doors for me that may not ever have been opened. Don't walk, SPRINT to get your sponsor training from Linda Hollander. You won't be disappointed–you will be inspired and empowered to new heights and possibilities!"

— **Heidi Garis, M.S.W., Business Owner and Coach**

her natural gifts to transfer her vast wealth of knowledge in the sponsorship arena and you will be fortunate to be able to take advantage of her warmth and expertise. She is a gem."

— **Mike Hayashi, M.Ed., Business Owner, Trainer and Media Expert**

"I didn't think a company would sponsor me, but Ocean Spray paid for my entire event."

— **Joanie Winberg, Speaker, Podcaster and Event Producer**

"Are you trying to reach corporate sponsors? Then go no further than the one and only Linda Hollander. She is a genius on how to connect with sponsors and media. In *Corporate Sponsorship in 3 Easy Steps*, Linda shares her expertise and provides the real tools you will need to grow your business!"

— **Janet Powers, Women's Toolbox**

"I teach Internet safety to families and my sponsors are funding my dreams."

— **Cynthia Frazier, Speaker and Business Owner**

"Because of Linda Hollander, we currently have several sponsors including major national companies. The information in *Corporate Sponsorship in 3 Easy Steps* is like gold to me!"

— **Linda Handley, Business Owner and Event Producer**

"Linda Hollander is brilliant! She is very knowledgeable and can help anyone craft their idea into a sponsor proposal that helps them build their business. Linda is very generous and the content you'll receive in this book is abundant and invaluable."

— **Brandy Amstel, Filmmaker and Business Owner**

"I've been in marketing departments my whole career and I thought I knew a little bit about this stuff, but I'm amazed at how much I didn't know that Linda Hollander knows. The information in this book is a tremendous value. I'm eternally grateful for Linda Hollander's knowledge and generosity."

— **Beverly Bergman, Marketing Business Owner**

"Linda Hollander is not only extremely knowledgeable, but without hesitation she shares the information about how to get sponsors to its fullest. Nothing is held back!"

— **Margaret Jackson, CEO of a Non-Profit Charity**

"Linda Hollander shares valuable knowledge that's not taught anywhere else that I know of. She's been in the trenches, made mistakes and can help you to propel forward without having to reinvent the wheel! The 'Wealthy Bag Lady' generously, candidly and honestly offers tips and secrets to help you succeed. I'm optimistic about my future in securing corporate sponsorships, thanks to this dynamo, Linda Hollander."

— **Jenny Robinson, Business Owner**

"Linda Hollander is a harbinger of possibilities, purpose, and prosperity. I love her voice in my ear and pithy reminders.

I dug up and aired buried dreams about getting sponsors when I read this book."

— **Vilasi Venkatachalam, Business Owner**

"Linda Hollander really gave me insight as to what is really possible in my life and career. Her enthusiasm and passion for helping others is second to none. I have never had a coach that was so 'hands-on' and there for me!"

— **Tami Lindahl, Certified Personal Trainer and Event Producer**

"Linda Hollander is like a light in the darkness! I now feel armed and ready to approach sponsors with confidence and establish great partnerships for my organization."

— **Lori Bell, CEO of a Non-Profit Charity**

"Linda is so accessible and has a huge heart to go with her excellent business sense and grasp of the realities of sponsorship. Her leadership is delightful - and a great model for other people who want to change the world."

— **Patricia Alexander, Speaker and Author**

"Linda Hollander is a dynamo. She not only delivers, she over-delivers. She really cares about you and will make sure you succeed."

— **Dr. Cynthia Barnett, Consultant and Event Producer**

"Linda Hollander is incredible and her genuine desire to serve is very inspirational to move you forward to reach your sponsorship goals. *Corporate Sponsorship in 3 Easy Steps* is a blueprint for success."

— **Elayna Fernandez,
CEO of a Non-Profit Charity**

"Linda Hollander is a first-class lady. She'll train you about how to get sponsors and her content is stellar."

— **Dr. Laureen Wishom, Positioning
and Business Growth Expert**

"If you want to get sponsors, have Linda Hollander mentor you. She really holds your hand and you'll be successful before you know it."

— **Liz Franklin, Productivity Coach
and Radio Host**

"Linda Hollander is the best! There's no one better at teaching business owners about the art of sponsorship and proposal writing."

— **Daniel Amis, Business Owner
and Relationship Coach**

"Look out Corporate America–my guns are loaded! *Corporate Sponsorship in 3 Easy Steps* gave me all the tools necessary in order to move forward getting the sponsorships needed for my business."

— **Liz Langsteiner, Business Owner**

CORPORATE SPONSORSHIP IN 3 EASY STEPS

Get Funding from Sponsors
Even if You're Just Getting Started

Linda Hollander

Corporate Sponsorship In 3 Easy Steps
Copyright © 2024 Linda Hollander

All rights reserved. This book or parts thereof may not be reproduced in any form, stored in a retrieval system or transmitted in any forms by any means. This includes, but is not limited to: electronic, mechanical, photocopy, recording, facsimile, or otherwise without the expressed written consent of the author, except as provided by United States of America Copyright law.

Edited by Jeannine Mallory
Cover and Interior Design by Fusion Creative Works

Address all inquiries to:
Linda Hollander
P.O. Box 83639
Los Angeles, CA 90083
310-337-1430
www.SponsorConcierge.com

ISBN: 978-1-940984-21-6
Library of Congress Control Number: 2014905118

Published by:
Aviva Publishing
Lake Placid, NY
518-523-1320
www.avivapubs.com

Acknowledgments

I don't know how it happened, but incredible people helped me grow this book from a fleeting fantasy into a reality. This book was truly a success team effort, made possible by the unwavering support of my family, friends, mentors, students, clients, and people like you who share my passion for sponsorship success.

I feel like I'm in Hollywood, accepting the Academy Award and desperately hoping I won't forget to mention any of the visionaries who helped make this book possible.

My first thank-you goes to my husband, Leslie Greenfield. He put up with my craziness, saw me at my worst, and continued to love me. I always wanted a great love in my life. Now I have one.

"Thank you" doesn't seem like enough for my best friend, Sheryl Felice. Your sacrifice and loyalty made it all possible. You held my vision in light. We are truly friends for life, and I cherish our friendship every day.

So many amazing people bring love and joy into my life. I would like to thank my parents, Robert and Blossom Hollander, for their love and support. You instilled wonderful values that have guided my life's choices. My "other parents," Howard and Rhoda Goldie, always pushed me toward my greatness. I couldn't ask for better role models. My beautiful and talented sister, Patricia Hollander, always encouraged me to be strong and go for my dreams. Every day, I hope to make you all proud of me.

Other members of my family have always supported me and shared their love: Steve and Monica Huss, Barbara Hartmann, James and Veronica Hartmann, Pablo Moline, Stella Moline, Camila Monchini, Pam Gibberman, and Curtis, Georgina, Matthew and Emily Shapiro. You are some of the most loving and courageous people I know.

I have the deepest admiration and gratitude for the members of my team: Cathy Fosco, who has the most beautiful heart; Jared Silver, one of the most talented and giving people I know; Maryann Baker, my constant cheerleader; and Alex Nghiem, a fountain of wisdom and a great mentor. This book would not have been possible without your constant support.

I've been blessed with many wonderful mentors. Sara Blakely, CEO and founder of Spanx, taught me to dream big and break down the obstacles in my path. Robert Allen ignited the spark that led to me becoming an author. Mark Victor Hansen taught me to think more creatively. I was blessed to see the beginning of the dream that became eWomen Network, by Kym and Sandra Yancey. Gina DeVee makes divine living an art. Suzanne Evans is a great "hell yeah" business mentor. Aggie Kobrin always saw the best in me and gave me great opportunities. Robbie Motter has inspired countless people with her winning spirit. Rhona Silver is smart, loyal, and talented. Al Lapin, Jr., founder of IHOP Restaurants, is an inspiration as a business maverick.

Many publishing mentors believed in me, provided support, and shared their wisdom with me. You are an author's dream, and I was truly lucky to find you. Your support breathed life into every page of this book. Patrick Snow is a book mentor extraordinaire. Shiloh Schroeder is a talented designer and Jeannine Mallory is an amazing book editor.

Being able to share laughs and chocolate with my girlfriends kept me sane throughout the crazy writing process. Heartfelt thanks go to my friends Diane Schoessow, Desiree Doubrox, and Rhonda Raider.

I had little furry writing companions including my beautiful cats, the dynamic mother-and-daughter duo, Carmella and Sneakers. My other favorite animals, Gigi, Buddy, Tuxedo, and Bailey, shower me with unconditional love whenever I visit. My spirit animals–Tuffy, Baya, Chelsea, Bo Jingles, Sundance, and Skippy–have also been loyal tail-waggin' pals.

Writing this book helped me fulfill my life's purpose to discover, motivate, and help sponsor seekers achieve their greatness. All the wonderful people who shared their stories with me inspired every page of this book. The Millionaire Mentors who shared their secrets have a true desire to empower others and make the world a better place. My clients and students have trusted me and let me into their lives. I learned so much from their experiences. Thank you all for your generosity and graciousness.

Finally, I would like to thank you, the reader, for believing that sponsorship can transform your life. If you would like to share your stories and comments, you can reach me at Sponsor Concierge, P.O. Box 83639, Los Angeles, CA 90083, 866-966-3624 or through my website, SponsorConcierge.com. Best of luck on your incredible journey!

Dedication

I am truly surrounded by love.

This book is dedicated to Bob and Blossom Hollander, my wonderful parents, for their love and support, to Leslie Greenfield, my loving husband, for sharing my vision and to Sheryl Felice, my best friend, for believing in the dream.

Table of Contents

INTRODUCTION   **25**
   Being a victim   26
   It's business. It's not personal   27
   My first success team   29
   The artist's path   29
   Wealthy Bag Lady   31
   My first sponsors   33
   My life after corporate sponsors   35

Sponsor Success Story: Susan G. Komen for the Cure   37
   Sponsors fulfilled a promise to her sister

Sponsor Success Story: Habitat for Humanity   38
   Sponsors providing homes to families

Sponsor Success Story: NASCAR   40
   Moving at the speed of sponsors

HOW TO USE THIS BOOK   **41**
   This book is about corporate sponsorships   41
   The sponsor secrets are for men and women   42
   For-profit and non-profit businesses can get sponsors   42
   I spend a lot of time convincing people that they can get sponsors   43
   Three-Step Process: Prepare, Propose and Promote   44
   I've made all the mistakes so you don't have to   47
   The sponsor strategies in this book are no-fluff and no-nonsense   48
   You're in the life-changing business   48
   Be prepared for negativity   49
   You need to fight for your dreams   52
   Do what you love and have a sponsor foot the bill   53

I.	**PREPARE**	**55**

Definition of Sponsorship	57
The Industry Definition of Sponsorship	57
Now Here's My Definition of Sponsorship	57
Cash Sponsors	58
In-Kind Sponsors	59
Commercial Potential	59
Your Property	60
Are They a Sponsor or a Partner?	60
Benefits of Corporate Sponsors	61
What Are the Advantages of Funding with Corporate Sponsors?	64
Avoid the cash flow roller coaster	64
Say goodbye to bounced checks and declined payments	64
Create profitable, life-changing events	65
Add creative funding for your dreams	65
How Do Sponsorships Compare with Other Kinds of Funding?	66
Joint Ventures	66
Loans	66
Credit Cards	67
Grants	67
Investors	68
What Sponsors Give You	69
Ways to Start Over Financially with No Credit Checks	69
Media and Public Relations Opportunities	69
Once-In-A-Lifetime Experiences	70
Your Chance to Peek Behind the Curtain	70
Who Qualifies for Corporate Sponsorships?	71
Small Business Owners and Social Entrepreneurs	71
Event Producers	71
Coaches and Consultants	72
Speakers, Authors and Self-Help Experts	72
Entertainment	73
Websites, Bloggers, Apps and Mobile Marketing	73
Media Personalities, Web TV, Radio and Podcasts	74
Sports and Athletes	75
Non-Profit Charities	75
Why Would a Company Sponsor You?	76
Increase brand loyalty	76

Create awareness and visibility	77
Change or reinforce image	78
Drive retail traffic	78
Grow their customer base	79
Open up a desirable geographic territory	79
Showcase community responsibility	80
Entertain clients	80
Recruit and retain employees	80
Direct connections with your target market	81
To be on your advisory board and connect with influential opinion leaders	81
Demonstrate category leadership	82
Opportunity to test a new product or service	82
To make people aware of a line extension	83
Damage control	83
Identification with a particular lifestyle	84
Enhance commitment to a diversity and ethnic groups	84
Drive sales!	85
Sponsor Success Story: Stars on Ice Skating on Sponsored Ice	86
What Sponsors Want	86
To know that you understand their goals	86
Demographics	87
Platform	87
Cause-Related Marketing Opportunities	88
Compelling Sponsor Proposal	88
Deliverables	88
Value	89
Integrity	89
Experience	89
Right of First Refusal	90
Follow Up	90
To Avoid Risk	90
Lead Time	91
Sponsor Success Story: Junior Achievement Sponsoring Youth to Build Businesses	92
Getting Sponsor Ready	93
Create Your Success Team	93
Types of Success Teams	94

Be clear about your property	97
Uplevel your web site and online presence	97
Make it easy for the sponsor to contact you	98
Be sure your all of your online branding is consistent	98
Make sure that your offline marketing materials brand you correctly	98
Build your audience	99
Get featured by the media	99
Start networking with people in Corporate America	101
Get training about corporate sponsorships	101
Start looking for a charitable partner	102
Don't make big demands of your charitable partner	103
Make a Sponsor Wish List	103
Top-Tier Sponsors	104
Second-Tier Sponsors	105
Love Brands	106
Out of Category Sponsors	106
Sponsor Success Story: Movember A Hairy Cause	108
Myths about Sponsorship	109
I need to be a non-profit.	109
I need to be in sports.	109
This is too sophisticated for me.	110
My business is too small.	110
I don't have enough experience.	111
I'm Independent. I don't want sponsors to influence me.	111
I'm not ready yet.	111
Biggest Mistakes People Make	112
Not asking for enough money	112
Putting the wrong benefits in their sponsor proposal	113
Making it all about you	113
Big file attachments	114
Unprofessional phone etiquette	114
Forgetting that integrity is part of your brand	115
Poor follow-up	116
Not having an industry-standard sponsor proposal	116
Corporate Sponsorship is Not Free Money or Get Rich Quick	117
Where to Find Sponsors	117
Internet	117

Trade shows	118
Events	118
Anyone interested in your property	119
Media campaigns	119
Directories	119
Social Media	120
Your Clients and Prospects	120
Research to Strengthen Your Sponsor Offering	**120**
Internet	121
Media kit	121
Universities	121
Hire a market research firm	121
Associations	121
Your surveys	122
Sponsors Pay You for Demographics	**122**
Age range and life-cycle stage	122
Gender mix	122
Educational background	123
Buying habits	123
Income range	123
Occupation	124
Socio-economic status	124
Marital and family status	124
Diversity	124
Psychographics	125
Building Your Audience	**125**
List-building web site	125
Collaborations	126
Public speaking	126
Events	127
Email marketing	127
Social media	128
Video marketing	128
Online and mobile marketing	129
Sponsor Benefits	**130**
Visibility	130
Connections and Engagement	132
Sponsor Success Story: South by Southwest Indie Goes Interactive	**140**

II. PROPOSE — 143

What's in a Sponsor Proposal? — 145
    Cover page — 147
    Goals for sponsors — 147
    Description of your property (executive summary) — 148
    Founder's story — 148
    Story of the property — 148
    Sponsor benefits — 148
    Demographics — 149
    Media opportunities — 149
    Marketing plan — 149
    Mission statement — 149
    Advisory board and strategic alliances — 150
    Testimonials — 150
    Sponsor levels and fees — 150
    Call to action — 150

Quick Facts Sheet — 151

How to Create Value — 151
    Value = Reach + Passion + Engagement — 151
    Think out of the box — 152
    I Hate Business Plans but I Love Sponsor Proposals — 152

Sponsor Success Story: Comic-Con — 153
    Comic Books Become Big Business

Paid, Owned and Earned Media — 154

Things in the Package That May Have — 155
Little Value to Sponsors

Sponsor Pet Peeves — 155
    Large attachments — 155
    Typos — 156
    Not doing your homework — 157
    Lying — 157
    Ramblers — 158
    Lack of authenticity — 159
    When they can't understand your property — 159
    Doing business with their competitors — 160

How to Contact Sponsors	160
Phone	160
In-Person	161
Email	161
Online Submissions	162
Direct Mail	162
Social Media	163
Sponsor Inquiry Form on Your Web Site	163
What Department of the Company Should You Contact for Sponsorship?	165
How to Talk to Sponsors	165
Lead with your compelling benefits	165
Be brief, be brilliant and be gone.	165
Make sure everyone on the sponsor's team is on the phone call	166
Always schedule a follow-up call and make sure everyone knows the next steps.	166
Send sponsor proposals electronically and by mail	167
Be prepared with a sponsor agreement	167
Get set up for payments from your sponsor	167
Keep everyone in the loop for more renewals	168
Have Telephone Scripts	168
Advisory Board and Strategic Alliances	168
Advisory Board and Management Team	169
Strategic Alliances	170
Testimonials	170
How to Get Testimonials	170
Charitable Causes and How They Can Help You	171
Should You Start Your Own Non-Profit?	172
Sponsor Success Story: First Book Magic of Reading for Children	173
Media Sponsors	174
Sponsor Strategy: Get Your Media Sponsors First	175
What's the difference between media sponsors and media appearances?	176

| III.   PROMOTE | 177 |

Get Content from Your Sponsors	180
Graphics	180
Videos	181
Copy	181
Surveys	181
Company Representatives	182
Other Information	182
Photograph and Document Everything	182
Seal the Deal and Get the Renewals	182
Sponsor Agreement	182
Sponsor Reports	183
Renewals	183
Support Your Sponsors	184
Sponsor Success Story: Alex's Lemonade Stand	185
Even a child can get sponsors	
Steps for Getting Your Sponsors	185
What Actions Will You Take?	188
Make your big dreams happen	189
Go for it	200
Author's Note	193

Introduction

"Success will be within your reach only when you start reaching out for it."

—**Stephen Richards**

I've led two lives: The life before and the life after I discovered corporate sponsors. Before I mastered the secrets of getting funding from corporate sponsors, I was limited to working from my kitchen table and not knowing how I was going to make my house payment. I had a powerful message, and I knew it would change the world, but I didn't know how I could reach people who needed to hear it. I didn't want to live an average life. I wanted my life to make a difference. I wanted to create a legacy.

I needed to live my life passionately and bravely, creating life-changing events and transforming lives. I wanted to provide for my family and friends and make sure they were successful in life.

I wanted to write books, travel, and get paid to speak in cities around the world. I imagined myself in exotic locations having phenomenal experiences and experiencing amazing food, art, and other cultures.

However, I didn't want to wait forever. I wanted to fast-track my wealth-creation and success by learning at the feet of the top business masters. I knew there was great information I could absorb like a sponge, and I wanted powerful partnerships.

I labored all day and into the night, but it seemed like I never got enough done. I was struggling **financially, physically,** and emotionally. My stress about paying the bills consumed my thoughts, so I couldn't even focus on my big dreams. I knew I was put on this earth for a purpose, but I was afraid I would die without fulfilling that mission. Every day was a struggle.

BEING A VICTIM

At the lowest point in my life, I was worse than broke because I was buried in major debt. I worked like a dog in a dead-end job to measure up to my boss's standard of performance. I battled the horrendous Los Angeles traffic just to get to the office. When I got there, I had to deal with trivial and nonsensical office politics and work with people I didn't like. I realized that to maintain my mental well-being, it was essential to surround myself with supportive people whom I liked and respected. I made up my mind that someday I would work with my dream team of people. I had an abrasive relationship with my boss, and the breaking point came when he said he was moving into my office. I couldn't imagine living in a fish bowl—especially with *him*—for eight hours each day. I had the spirit of an entrepreneur, and my soul was crying out.

IT'S BUSINESS. IT'S NOT PERSONAL.

I talked to my friends about my unhappiness with the people I worked with and they advised me to "suck it in." It was "just business." I shouldn't take it personally when there was backstabbing, lack of respect, and open hostility toward me.

But my work *is* personal. It's where I spend most of my time, brainstorm ideas, and work for a common goal. I needed a supportive environment in my workplace and my primary relationships.

During the workday, I usually had lunch by myself. The loneliness was devastating and my spirit was crushed. During this time, I was afraid to go to my own mailbox. My hand would actually shake when I held the mailbox key. I hoped every month that I'd be able to pay rent and that my old car wouldn't break down. Because of my overwhelming debt, I knew I could not afford to pay certain bills. Because I wasn't making enough money at my job, I maxed out my credit cards. As a result, credit card companies and debt collectors constantly harassed me on the phone. My bills were always there, mocking me, as a constant reminder of my financial failures.

I lived in a low-rent apartment, and my only "family" was my beautiful cat, Tuffy. One day my landlord saw the cat and demanded that I get rid of my furry little friend. Tuffy was the most precious thing in my life and there was no way I was going to give him up. I concealed the innocent little feline from my landlord and I was constantly worried about being discovered. I couldn't afford to live anywhere else, so I had no other choice. I couldn't even imagine buying a home of my own.

In my personal life, I was dating a temperamental and abusive man. He was not a batterer. There was never any physical abuse, but there was plenty of mental anguish. When we first met, he called me constantly, sent me flowers, and proclaimed his love for me. But as the relationship progressed, he exhibited his darker side. He was prone to tremendous mood swings. After a while, I didn't know what would set off his ugly temper. He also became jealous of the time I spent with my girlfriends. I knew I would never fully commit to him. I did not want to be doomed to a miserable life. Unfortunately, my self-confidence was so low that I thought this relationship was better than no relationship at all. Without this man, I thought I'd be doomed to a life of loneliness. I was a single woman who knew I had to take care of myself. I never had any illusions of being supported by a man.

But I wasn't willing to settle for an average life. I didn't want to be a victim or a cog in someone else's machine. I wanted more. I didn't believe we were put on this earth to work our fingers to the bone and never see the light at the end of the tunnel.

MY FIRST SUCCESS TEAM

In some ways, the story of my life began when I was 13 years old. I was on the playground at recess when one of my classmates, Sheryl Felice, asked me to have lunch with her. We didn't know it at the time, but the unstoppable girl-power that has guided our lives was officially set into motion that day. We began creating the ultimate success team.

Sheryl and I have been a force to be reckoned with ever since that day on the school playground. We are closer than sisters are, and we have gone through incredible life experiences together. According to motivational speaker and author Terri Murphy, "Friends are the gems in the jewelry box of life." Whenever a boyfriend dumped me or an idiot boss spewed out his venom on me, Sheryl was a comforting shoulder to cry on. When something momentous happened in my life, she was there to share in the excitement.

THE ARTIST'S PATH

As a child, I loved to draw and paint. This passion and talent continued well into my teenage years. Everyone who saw my artwork encouraged me to become a professional artist. My mother encouraged me to become an artist, but my father was more practical about how I would earn a living. Being an artist would probably relegate me to a meager existence. I would be constantly worried about money. Every freelance job would be another proving ground for me and my talent. I would never know financial security.

For most of my life, I thought business was boring. I never took one business class in college. All of my university studies were in art. I wanted to make a total commitment to developing my craft.

Art was the perfect career choice for me because it let me hide from the world. I was painfully shy and did not mind the oppression of "studio life." Being alone all day to paint my large canvases and collages was wonderful. For me, stressful situations were parties, job interviews, blind dates, and even getting my hair done, because I had to make conversation with people. I was the kid in the back of the classroom who was constantly hiding and in fear of raising my hand. Being invisible, my schoolteachers would never remember me. I didn't even start dating until I was in my twenties.

After college, my work was accepted into some art exhibitions. I sold some paintings, but had only enough money to go to the grocery store...*once*. I wanted to do some strange things, like eat, buy clothing, pay rent...and breathe. A gallery position in sales was the answer. My first sale was the ultimate high. I realized I could actually develop a rapport with people and convince them to buy something. I learned the techniques of prospecting, building relationships, and closing. At this time, management was starting to recognize my abilities. One day, the manager, Mike, said to me, "Kiddo, I like the way you handle your customers. Even if an art piece is $25,000, you say 'It's only $25,000.' It actually turns the conversation away from price and onto the benefits."

WEALTHY BAG LADY

Being an artist, I collected shopping bags with cool graphics. One day, my mother called and said she was coming to my little apartment. I picked up the shopping bags and tried to put them away, but the closet was overstuffed, and the bags cascaded down on me. You could say that the idea for my shopping bag business literally "hit me on the head."

Then, with my cat on my lap, I called my best friend Sheryl and asked if she wanted to take the biggest adventure ride of our lives and start a business together. Luckily, she said yes.

We started one of the only women-owned businesses that printed shopping bags, and soon we had clients like Disney, Sears, Nissan, and Mattel. I always loved helping small businesses. Women business owners came to our company and we didn't just do business together. They asked me how to do sales and marketing and I shared business-building strategies with them. One of my customers said, "You're not just a bag lady. You're a wealthy bag lady." I knew this was my brand because I got chills when she said it.

I learned about business by trial and error, and I found out that trial and error can be expensive, in both money and time. I realized I liked making money more than losing it. Through talking to many successful business owners and millionaires, I learned their business secrets.

When I started my own business, I was thrust into an entirely different world. Instead of dog-eat-dog, it was dog-*help*-dog.

When I went to forums with entrepreneurs, people made sure to introduce me to people who could help me, either by becoming mentors or customers. I did the same for them and loved being a business matchmaker.

I went to so many seminars that I was called the "seminar queen." If there was a conference about real estate, investing or business, I was there. I met the man of my dreams at one of these seminars. He was one of the kindest people I ever met and he became a constant source of love and support. We are now happily married and Leslie is the best man I've ever known.

I moved out of my small rent-controlled apartment and bought my first home as a single woman. The home-buying process was terrifying and exhilarating at the same time. I had gone from a small rent-controlled apartment to a home of my own. I could leave all the lights on if I wanted to decorate and, most of all, have my cat without hiding or being afraid of ending up on the streets. Signing the closing papers and receiving the house key was the ultimate high. I discovered a love of gardening and planting my home garden created a special bond between my mother and me.

Positive things began to happen in my life when I made the decision to strike out on my own and start my business. By learning the secrets to running a successful small business, I went from being a victim to being the master of my own life. Now it was my turn to become a mentor.

My consulting business was born. My clients said I should write a book, so I wrote *Bags to Riches: 7 Success Secrets for Women in Business*. Then I did a media and speaking tour for my book. I met women business owners around the country. It was all great fun. These women told me they wanted an empowerment forum where they could get gems of advice from the top business experts in the world. The idea for the Women's Small Business Expo was born.

The Women's Small Business Expo became my entire world. It was the first thing I thought about when I woke up in the morning and the last thing I thought about before I laid my head on the pillow at night.

I was terrified. I knew I was fulfilling my purpose to empower women through entrepreneurial success, but I had no experience in planning events. The Women's Small Business Expo was cash-intensive and risky. I had never done an event in my life, and I had to reserve hotel rooms, hire speakers, book talent, plan menus, and risk lots of money. I didn't even know if anyone was going to show up. What if I gave a great party and nobody came?

MY FIRST SPONSORS

I needed a way to fund my dreams of the Women's Small Business Expo. That's when the idea of corporate sponsors came to me. I'd noticed other women's business conferences had something amazing called "sponsors." I was still the seminar queen, so I attended as many of these events as

I could. I saw how they promoted their sponsors and how they recognized them from the platform. Some of them even acknowledged that the event would not have been possible without their sponsors. Who were these magical companies?

I knew I needed sponsors to pay for the Women's Small Business Expo. I didn't let my lack of experience, the fact that I had no guaranteed audience, or even my checkbook balance get in my way. I was a woman on a mission.

I hired a company to create an amazing sponsor proposal and then I set out to get my first sponsors. After submitting a sponsor proposal to Bank of America and having a few conversations, they requested a meeting. I was thrilled and terrified. When I'm scared, I turn to music. Girl-power songs gave me the shot of courage I needed. On the way to my meeting with Bank of America, I blasted "I Will Survive" by Gloria Gaynor in my car. My dreams of sponsorship could actually come true. But I could also fail publicly. I could walk away from the meeting feeling victorious or rejected.

Steve from Bank of America was behind the desk when I sat down. I handed him a copy of my sponsor proposal and I went over each page of it. Instinctively, I'd brought extra copies in case he needed to show it to other members of his team. My legs were crossed, so he couldn't see my knees shaking. After I answered his questions, he said, "We'll be happy to go with the sponsorship." I accepted this as if I did it all the time, while inside I wanted to scream for joy! I behaved professionally for the rest of the meeting and asked him what the next steps were. Then I shook his hand and told him I looked forward to having Bank of America as my sponsor. Woo-hoo!

It seemed like forever before I got into my car and finally expressed my excitement. When I was finally alone, I screamed and did a happy dance. Then I sat there for a moment to take in the enormity of what just happened. I had turned an idea in my head into something other people could actually get excited about and invest in.

After Bank of America, IBM, WalMart, Microsoft, Citibank, FedEx, Health Net, American Airlines, Staples and more, became sponsors. I couldn't believe it. Even though I made many mistakes, leading-edge companies validated my sponsorship offering. My dreams of stepping into my greatness, creating a legacy, and empowering women were actually about to happen.

MY LIFE AFTER CORPORATE SPONSORS

Sponsors helped me make the Women's Small Business Expo possible. Through this empowerment event, entrepreneurs created multimillion-dollar partnerships. Women were able to build great businesses, provide for their families, and send their kids to good schools. Their dreams took flight.

I received notes from women saying they were able to get out of bad relationships because, after hearing my story, they took back their power and refused to be victims. This led to me speaking all over the country, doing lots of media interviews, traveling, and creating an amazing life, all because of corporate sponsors.

I met the greatest business leaders of our time and was mentored by them. Amazing people contacted me, wanting to do powerful collaborations. I gave money to charities that taught entrepreneurship to kids, rescued animals, won awards, and helped women survive domestic abuse. I even got to judge a contest where students created real working companies, complete with professional presentations.

Working with sponsors gave me the chance to peek behind the curtain and see how "Corporate America" really works. I listened to their conversations about money. Key influencers actually took my calls. I learned the marketing strategies of "big money" and applied them to my own small business.

I traveled the world. I swam above Australia's Great Barrier Reef, marveled at the Acropolis in Athens, kissed the Blarney Stone in Ireland, tasted the wine in Italy, and saw Paris from the Eiffel Tower.

Now I have a new mission: To empower you to use the awesome power of corporate sponsors. With the resources sponsors provide, you can live your passionate life and do it bravely. You have the power to create your future.

SPONSOR SUCCESS STORY: SUSAN G. KOMEN FOR THE CURE

Sponsors fulfilled a promise to her sister

Nancy G. Brinker promised her dying sister, Susan G. Komen, that she would do everything in her power to end breast cancer forever. Nancy told her husband she wanted to start a non-profit organization for breast cancer and started working out of her garage. Her husband was supportive. He just asked her not to contact any of their friends and ask them for money. As soon as he left the house, Nancy started soliciting every one of their friends for donations.

Those humble beginnings and Nancy's promise to her sister grew into Susan G. Komen for the Cure®, and it launched the global breast cancer movement. Today, Susan G. Komen is the boldest community, fueling the best science and making the biggest impact in the fight against breast cancer. Thanks to events like the Komen Race for the Cure, more than $2 billion has been invested in the promise of working to end breast cancer in the U.S. and the world through groundbreaking research, community health outreach, advocacy, and programs in more than 50 countries.

They have provided more early detection and effective treatment options for women. Currently, about 70 percent of women 40 and older get mammograms, thermography, and ultrasounds to find breast cancer early. Since 1990, there has been a 33 percent decline in breast cancer mortality in the U.S. The five-year relative survival rate for women diagnosed with early stage breast cancer is now 98 percent. Currently, there are more than three million breast cancer survivors, the largest group of cancer "thrivers" in the U.S.

The Komen Organization quickly realized that corporate sponsors were keys to building their tiny charity into a worldwide movement. Komen partners have included American Airlines, Ford, New Balance, ReMax Realty, Walgreens, Bank of America, Georgia Pacific, Stanley Steemer, and Energizer.

"No person was ever honored for what he received. Honor is given by what he gave."

– Calvin Coolidge

SPONSOR SUCCESS STORY: HABITAT FOR HUMANITY

Sponsors providing homes to families

Habitat for Humanity was originally referred to as "Habitat for Insanity." It was founded by Millard and Linda Fuller in 1976.

In 1984, former U.S. President Jimmy Carter and his wife Rosalynn took their first Habitat work trip. They fell in love with the cause and their personal involvement in Habitat for Humanity brought the organization international visibility. Habitat for Humanity experienced a dramatic increase in the number of new affiliates around the country.

Today Habitat for Humanity helps those in need find new hope in the form of affordable housing. Habitat builds and repairs houses all over the world using volunteer labor and donations. Partner families purchase these houses through no-profit, no-interest mortgage loans or innovative financing methods. Since the organization began in 1976, Habitat for Humanity has helped provide shelter for more than 750,000 families and helped more than three million people around the world.

At the beginning, they practically had to beg people to be volunteers for their home-building teams. Now, there is a waiting list to be on a building team for a Habitat for Humanity house. It's a great way to do team-building for a company and you meet influential people on the work crews.

Thanks to corporate sponsors such as Lowe's, Time Warner, Bank of America, Citibank, Nissan, Whirlpool, and Folgers, Habitat for Humanity has become a world leader in addressing poverty and providing housing for the needy.

> "There is no dishonor in losing the race. There is only dishonor in not racing because you are afraid to lose."
>
> **—Garth Stein**

SPONSOR SUCCESS STORY: NASCAR

Moving at the speed of sponsors

The National Association for Stock Car Auto Racing (NASCAR) is a family-owned and operated business venture that sanctions and governs multiple auto racing sports events. Bill France Sr. founded it in Daytona Beach, Florida in 1948. His father was a teller at Park Savings Bank in Washington, and his son might have followed his example. However, Bill France was fascinated with automobiles and how they performed.

Over the years, NASCAR's corporate sponsors have included Sprint, Nextel, Toyota, Nationwide Insurance, Camping World, 3M, Breyers Ice Cream, Chevrolet, Coors Light, M&Ms, Ragu, Sherwin Williams, UPS, and Visa.

Because of corporate sponsors, NASCAR is the largest sanctioning body of stock car racing in the America. In terms of television ratings, NASCAR is second only to the National Football League among professional sports organizations.

How to Use This Book

"Take the first step, and your mind will mobilize all its forces to your aid. But the first essential is that you begin. Once the battle is started, all that is within and without you will come to your assistance."

—Robert Collier

THIS BOOK IS ABOUT CORPORATE SPONSORSHIPS

In this book, we'll talk about corporate sponsorship for your business, event, non-profit or project. Other forms of "sponsorship" won't be discussed here. Politicians sponsor bills and 12-step programs such as Alcoholics Anonymous have sponsors.

At some events, speakers who pay a fee to do their presentations are called sponsors. Sometimes companies who contribute to conference gift bags are called sponsors. Some events refer to their exhibitors as sponsors. Advertisers on the Internet are often called sponsors.

Corporate sponsorship may include these elements, but there's much more to it. It takes about as much effort to sell small advertising, such as a display ad or listing on your web site, as it does to get major sponsorships. There's a greater possibility of long-term successful benefits in corporate sponsorships.

THE SPONSOR SECRETS ARE FOR MEN AND WOMEN

I have more than 20 years of experience with women business owners. Some people know me for my Women's Small Business Expo events or the brand of "Wealthy Bag Lady."

Occasionally, I'll use the women's market as examples in this book because of my background, but the secrets of getting sponsors are universal. They work for men and women. Sponsorship can help you regardless of your gender, age, income, ethnicity, occupation, education, or experience.

FOR-PROFIT AND NON-PROFIT BUSINESSES CAN GET SPONSORS

One of the biggest myths is that you need to be a non-profit organization to get corporate sponsors. I've always been a for-profit business and many of my clients are profit-driven. As a for-profit business, project or event, you can be successful with corporate sponsors. In fact, sponsors want you to make a profit. They know that if you understand the basics of business, then you'll handle their money well. You'll be around for the long haul to promote their company.

Of course, non-profits can also get sponsors and savvy charities are flush because they've mastered the art of corporate sponsorship. The best non-profits don't get caught up in egos and poverty mentality. They run their organizations with strong business principles so they don't go out of business. The more money you have, the more people you can help.

I SPEND A LOT OF TIME CONVINCING PEOPLE THAT THEY CAN GET SPONSORS

"I always pass on good advice. It is the only thing to do with it. It is never of any use to oneself."

—Oscar Wilde

Some people also think they can't get sponsors if they're just starting out. When I got my first top-tier sponsors, I didn't have any following, financing, or experience. However, I was willing to learn.

A common trait of successful people is that they are teachable. Approach the information about sponsors with the wide-eyed innocence of a child. Instead of thinking, "This doesn't apply to me," think about how you can use the strategies here to catapult your success. I'll be sharing some sponsor success stories. These people and properties (persons or entities seeking sponsorship) started with nothing but a vision and grew into something that influenced many people's lives. Instead of thinking that these properties are so much bigger than where you are right now, see how you can learn from their journeys. I'll also share stories of people like you, so you'll know you can get sponsors even if you don't have an audience or experience.

3-STEP PROCESS: PREPARE, PROPOSE AND PROMOTE

"Be prepared, work hard, and hope for a little luck. Recognize that the harder you work and the better prepared you are, the more luck you might have."

—Ed Bradley

People call me every day and tell me that they think sponsorship is too complicated and sophisticated for them. I've divided the sponsorship process into three easy steps:

1. Prepare
2. Propose
3. Promote

PREPARE

The "Prepare" section of this book is the largest because, without the right preparation, potential sponsors will reject you, and you'll miss some great opportunities. You'll experience an exercise in frustration. You won't even know why, because sponsors don't usually tell you the reason they rejected you.

Even if you're chomping at the bit to get your sponsors, spend some time learning and preparing. It could mean the difference between success and failure in the sponsor game.

Preparation also inspires confidence. You'll be able to approach and talk to your sponsors with aplomb.

Preparation includes your inner and outer game. The inner game is your mindset and I'll tell you how to train your brain for success. Your brain gives you a multitude of messages each day. Unfortunately, many of these messages are negative self-talk. There may also be bad data in your mind that was programmed from childhood that needs to be replaced with good programming. In other words, you may be operating from a life script that just isn't working for you anymore. This is also known as the "shadow mind" and it's the reason people self-sabotage just before they hit their stride. Why not use the amazing power of your brain for positive self-talk?

The outer game is the strategies for getting sponsors. I'll tell you how sponsors can help you, the advantages of sponsorships over other types of funding, how to qualify for corporate sponsorships, why a company would want to sponsor you, and how to groom yourself for corporate sponsors.

PROPOSE

I'll share what goes into an industry-standard sponsor proposal. Without the right sponsor proposal, don't even bother to go after sponsors. If a sponsor receives a proposal that is not at industry-standard level, it will be rejected, and you may not be able to re-submit to that sponsor. I want you to have every advantage in the sponsor world. The sponsor proposal is also called the *prospectus* and the *sponsor deck*. There are specific ways to create value and you'll find out how to contact the "make-it-happen" person. When it's time to talk to sponsors, you need to use a certain language. Your first conversation is like an audition and your sponsor will have you pass certain tests. Have I made you nervous yet? Don't worry. I'll share all the insider secrets with you.

PROMOTE

When you sign the contract and make the deal with your sponsor, it's only the beginning. Don't just use your sponsor's resources and then forget them. You would be surprised by the number of people who collect the sponsor fee and then come back with their hand outstretched for more money after a year. Imagine what the sponsor is thinking at that point. The sponsor wants to know what you've done for them all year.

After you negotiate your sponsorship deal, it's time to promote your sponsor and create a great rapport so you can get the renewal for the next contract period. Sponsorship is a relationship business and you'll want to keep the lines of communication open. Photograph, video, and document everything you do for your sponsor. Call, email, text, and communicate with them regularly to let them know you're fulfilling your contract and adding value to their company. If you communicate properly with your sponsor, then the renewal is the most natural thing in the world.

I MADE ALL THE MISTAKES, SO YOU DON'T HAVE TO

"You must be big enough to admit your mistakes, smart enough to profit from them, and strong enough to correct them."

—John C. Maxwell

I'm not providing these sponsor strategies as some sort of exalted high authority. I've made all the mistakes and more. I've sent out sponsor proposals with major typos, bad graphics, terrible layouts, and the wrong benefits. I had no idea how much money to ask for and what to do when I got the sponsor's money. I was terrified that sponsors would find out I didn't know what I was doing.

Sponsors and other professionals caught some of my mistakes. They were great learning experiences and I'll share them with you. Other blunders went unnoticed by my sponsors, but I caught and corrected them.

I've left lots of money on the table because I didn't know how to approach sponsors and what to do once I got them. I spent more than $75,000 and six months on my first sponsor proposal because of all the mistakes I made. In fact, just changing one word in the sponsor proposal made the difference between success and failure in one deal.

THE SPONSOR STRATEGIES IN THIS BOOK ARE NO-FLUFF AND NO-NONSENSE

I know you're a leader and your time is valuable, so I'm giving you real-world advice that comes from experience. If I say something that sounds harsh or makes you uncomfortable, please know that my advice comes from my desire for you to succeed with your sponsors. If you've already made one of the classic mistakes, don't worry. Just change what didn't work move on. Mistakes can be more valuable than successes because people remember their blunders vividly and they don't make the same mistake twice. Think of me as a trusted friend who is looking out for you and wants to give you all of the advantages in the sponsor game. Sponsorship is a game and I'll give you the rules.

Don't think of sponsorship as free money. The ideal sponsor relationship is a true win-win partnership. You and your sponsor both receive great benefits.

If you're looking for excuses about why you can't get sponsors, you've come to the wrong place. I've blown all the excuses out of the water. You'll see how people just like you, even children, have attracted great sponsors, even when they had no audience and no experience.

YOU'RE IN THE LIFE-CHANGING BUSINESS

"There's lots of bad reasons to start a company. But there's only one good, legitimate reason, and I think you know what it is: it's to change the world."

—Phil Libin, Evernote

Whatever it is, if you're a for-profit business, a non-profit charity, an event, an entertainer, an online property, or a sports promoter, or you have a special project, you're in the life-changing business. You are a true innovator. You have created something that is going to change and transform people's lives. When people's lives are changed, they transform others, just as a pebble creates ripples in the water. When you are on your true mission, you'll have an infectious life force. You can create powerful change.

BE PREPARED FOR NEGATIVITY

Even though you're in the life-changing business, when you announce your intentions to get sponsors, your family and friends, even your business colleagues, may not always respond with enthusiasm.

They may say, "Don't you know you need to be a big business to get sponsors? Why would a company sponsor you?"

Going in a new direction requires courage. You must protect your fragile dreams in their early stages. The media gives us the impression that gigantic forces outside ourselves, such as the economy, thwart our dreams. In reality, the danger lies much closer. Instead of being your allies, your friends, family, and colleagues may be critical and cause you to question your dreams.

Your friends and family are not trying to throw a wet blanket on your fire because they are cruel. They care about you and they don't want to see you fail or get hurt. The role of the trailblazer can be lonely. Fear of the unknown is universal. Human beings are creatures of habit and, by nature, afraid of change. Getting sponsors requires a huge change in thoughts and actions.

When Estée Lauder started her cosmetics business, her attorney and her accountant took her out to dinner. The dinner turned into an intervention. They told her that the skincare game was brutal. It would chew her up and spit her out. She listened to these men, who were professionals, much older and more experienced than she was. And she almost quit. Then she remembered her love of cosmetics and skincare and her passion for selling "hope in a jar." She knew women would hold off on buying the latest dress, but they would always spend money on their faces. She created an international cosmetics empire. In the end, she was right.

Sara Blakely, founder of Spanx, told me that she didn't tell other people about her business for the first year because she didn't want to hear any negative thoughts. Spanx is a line of shapewear and pantyhose that is actually comfortable for women. When Sara went to see her first patent attorney, she noticed that his eyes were darting all around his office. He didn't even look at her. After the meeting, he admitted that he thought her idea was so stupid that he must have been on a hidden camera show. Sara Blakely went on to get Neiman Marcus as one of her first customers and became one of the youngest female billionaires in America.

For me, the naysayer was my father. When I started my bag business, I had a terrible fight with him. My father is 5'6" but to me, he was always larger than life. His tiny shoes were too big to fill. I love my father dearly and I needed his approval more than anything in the world. I didn't get it. I had two failed businesses and art school training. My father told me I was a dreamer "living in a fantasy world." How dare I even think I could start a business?

His words were like daggers to me. The rift with my father lasted for a year. It hurt me to the core of my being and left a tremendous hole in my heart.

I made a decision. I could believe him, take his words to heart, or I could show him that he was wrong about me. I knew it was my time to strike out on my own, so I built my business and traveled the world.

Life was great, but I was missing the one thing: My father's approval. I started teaching small business success seminars. I sent an audio of one of my classes to my father.

Then one day I got a phone call. It was a gruff, familiar voice. My father made a special call to tell me he was proud of me. He apologized for all the hurtful things he'd said in the past. I felt so much love, that I thought my heart would burst. Now my father and I have a great relationship. He is my biggest fan and we've been close ever since.

If you're not surrounded by positive people who support you, then it's time to find a new group. Assemble a power team to support you and hold your visions in light. They don't always need to agree with you. In fact, they should challenge you. This stalwart crew will become your advisory board. They will help you grow, do what you love, and get great sponsors.

YOU NEED TO FIGHT FOR YOUR DREAMS

"Every great dream begins with a dreamer. Always remember, you have within you the strength, the patience, and the passion to reach for the stars to change the world."

—Harriet Tubman

I've broken the process of sponsorship down into easy steps, but it will involve work. You can either do the work yourself or hire a company to do it for you. Ask any self-made successful person and you'll find out that it took lots of hard work. People thought they were crazy, rebellious dreamers. Successful people did things other people were not willing to do and took risks that would terrify most people. Even if they didn't have much money, they found ways to invest in themselves.

I've worked with FedEx as a sponsor. I learned that when the founder, Fred Smith, presented the business plan for FedEx in college at Yale, his professor told him it was not feasible.

Today, the world is grateful that Smith didn't let someone else's opinion stop him from achieving his dream.

DO WHAT YOU LOVE AND HAVE A SPONSOR FOOT THE BILL

"I knew that if I failed I wouldn't regret that, but I knew the one thing I might regret is not trying."

—Jeff Bezos, Amazon Founder and CEO

I feel like I know you. You have big dreams. You have a message that needs to get out because it will change people's lives. You want to create a legacy that you can pass on to future generations. You want to help people and you want to make money while you're doing it. You want to live well and help your family and friends succeed in life. You've also had some obstacles. There have been people who didn't believe in you. You've had bad advice, possibly health issues in your family, and even struggles with money. Despite these obstacles, you knocked down roadblocks and created some accomplishments in your life.

Now you need to realize your dreams and go for your greatness! It's not even a choice anymore. This is your time. Your "someday" is now.

We've been taught to go for our dreams, but it takes money and the right connections to fund those dreams. You can only go so far on your own with limited funds. That's where corporate sponsors come in. Let's start now.

I. Prepare

Success occurs when preparation meets opportunity, so we'll spend a lot of time on the *Prepare* section of sponsorship. I know you're excited to get started, but the more time you put into preparing your sponsorship action plan, the more successful you'll be with your sponsors. Let's start out with some vocabulary and definitions.

DEFINITION OF SPONSORSHIP

THE INDUSTRY DEFINITION OF SPONSORSHIP

Corporate sponsorship is a cash and/or in-kind fee paid to a property in return for access to the commercial potential associated with that property.

NOW HERE'S MY DEFINITION OF SPONSORSHIP

Sponsors give you money and resources to connect them with people who buy things.

I'll illustrate this with an example:

A very nice woman named Rose called me with a request to help her get books to prisoners. Many prisoners are released back into society, so I liked the idea of this program. Although it was a great and noble pursuit, she did not qualify for sponsorships because prisoners are not consumers. They do not buy things. Rose went on to get funding through grants and foundation money, but her property wasn't appropriate for sponsors.

You need to know people who buy things, and how your sponsor can connect with them. These are your *demographics*. The more compelling your demographics are to your sponsors, the more successful you'll be with your corporate sponsors.

Think about the most successful sponsorships. There's NASCAR, where sponsors pay beaucoup bucks to be connected to people who buy all kinds of services and consumer goods. This group likes to buy from the companies who sponsor the racecar drivers, automobiles, uniforms and hats. The racecar drivers look like walking billboards for their sponsor companies.

Let's talk about more sponsor vocabulary.

CASH SPONSORS

Cash sponsorship is also known as hard dollars. This is a cash payment in exchange for adding value to your sponsor by marketing, goodwill, tangible and intangible benefits. Cash sponsorship comes in the form of a physical check, transfer, electronic funds or credit cards. We all need cash for our businesses, events, non-profits and projects, and you can also find value with in-kind sponsors.

IN-KIND SPONSORS

In-kind sponsors are also called trade sponsors or soft dollars. You'll find tremendous value with in-kind sponsors because they are budget-relieving. My clients have received free food, beverage, printing, event locations, cars and flights. With in-kind sponsors, one of the biggest benefits is "free stuff."

The ultimate big daddy of in-kind sponsorships is media. I've received $25,000 of radio advertising without a dime coming out of my pocket. This included 30-second spots, 60-second spots, advertising on the radio station web site, and sponsor spotlights. The radio station even helped me write the commercial, and had their top talent read the copy. Then they edited the radio spot and even added a soundtrack.

Sometimes it's not just a choice of in-kind or cash sponsorships. You can do both. Some sponsor deals include some cash and some amazing in-kind benefits. Let sponsors know you're willing to work with them. Think out of the box and get creative in your sponsor deals.

COMMERCIAL POTENTIAL

Sponsors need a way to make money. This is called the commercial potential. It comes from various aspects of your property, such as connections to your target demographic, cause marketing, media, promotions, interactive campaigns, engagement, and goodwill. Sponsors need a return on their investment and a return on their objectives. Companies have long-term and short-term goals and they need to make money to keep their business running, answer to their stockholders, and keep good team members.

YOUR PROPERTY

Your property is the entity available for sponsorship. When sponsorship first began, physical properties, such as stadiums and arenas, were sponsored. Just think of the local sports arenas and concert stadiums where you live. Which ones are sponsored?

Now, you can be sponsored as a person, business, non-profit, or other entity. Think of celebrity doctors, athletes, chefs, and business leaders who get endorsement deals from sponsors. This is lucrative work and you can do it. Your property can also be your business, book, brand, speaking tour, event, show, sports team, charity or project. Another term for someone seeking sponsorship is the sponsee or rights holder.

ARE THEY A SPONSOR OR A PARTNER?

Some companies prefer the term "sponsor," and some prefer "partner." Mix up the terms in your sponsor proposal and pitch letter so they will be comfortable with your terminology. You can also call it "sponsorship marketing." The term "partner" can mean so many things. It can mean two people who do business together and divide the profits. It could be a limited joint venture, investor relationship, etc. The word "sponsor" is more specific, so I'll use that term in this book.

BENEFITS OF CORPORATE SPONSORS

Here are the top benefits of getting funding from corporate sponsors:

1. Money

Sponsors give you money so you can do what you love and change people's lives. The most successful businesses have multiple sources of income. Knowing that your sponsor fees will come continually is a game-changer. This revenue lets you play at a higher level. You can achieve celebrity status, help more people, and dream bigger. You can also use sponsor fees to expand your team, make purchases for your property, and launch marketing campaigns. Savvy non-profits have also mastered the art of corporate sponsor funding.

2. Resources and Media

Sponsors don't always give you money, but they will give you in-kind sponsorships and trade benefits. This includes food and beverage for events, travel, printing of marketing materials, and the biggest in-kind sponsor benefit: media. Media sponsorship allows you to get the word out about your property, your event, book, charity, show, association, projects or business without any money out of pocket. Such media include traditional as well as new media and they offer fast track to success.

3. Credibility

Having sponsors gives you more credibility in your industry and community. When people see "sponsored by" and the names of leading-edge companies on your web site, social media, and marketing materials, your credibility will shoot through the roof. This fast track to a stellar reputation took years to build in the past. Now you have more authority and visibility in the marketplace. Having sponsors telegraphs to people that you're playing at a higher level, which helps you get more clients, donors, event attendees, and more sponsors. There's a lot of "me too" in the sponsor world, so one sponsor leads to another.

4. More Clients

There is a simple rule in business: If you want to be successful, hang out with successful people. People pay lots of money to travel to high-level networking events. I do it regularly. The right collaborations and referrals can change your business and your life. Having sponsors helps you get more clients and referrals.

5. Exposure

Sponsors can also promote you with their colleagues, employees, and customers. You can reap the benefits of their public relations firms and expert marketing. Leading-edge companies have top-notch marketing and promotion teams that you may not be able to get access to on your own. Sponsorship gives you access to the top talent and brainpower of these public relations wunderkinds and you get an insider's view of how big money operates. Nobody wants to be the best-kept secret and funding from sponsors helps you acquire more exposure on a larger scale.

6. Renewals

One of the most awesome things about corporate sponsorships is renewals. After you get your sponsors, you can get renewals again and again. I recommend a one-year contract with a one-year renewal. This means that you get the sponsor fee for the one-year contract and then they can give you money for the next year. I've had many clients who have received multi-year contracts from their sponsors. I've also enjoyed long-term relationships with my sponsor companies. Sponsor renewals allow you to create profitable relationships and fund your dreams. Sponsorship is a relationship business, so keep in touch with your sponsors all year. Then you'll be more successful with renewals.

7. Ability to Help More People

The more money you have, the more people you can help. We're all taught to have big dreams, but we're not taught how to fund those dreams. That's where corporate sponsors come in. They give wings to your goals and visions. You can help other people step into their greatness. You're in the life-changing business and sponsorship gives you the resources to help more people and change more lives.

WHAT ARE THE ADVANTAGES OF FUNDING WITH CORPORATE SPONSORS?

> *"The money is out there, and countless institutions have secured funding and enjoyed many happy years with their sponsors."*
>
> **– Matthew Caines**

AVOID THE CASH FLOW ROLLER COASTER

As business owners, we ride the entrepreneurial roller coaster. Some months, the money rolls in. You get clients and life is good. Birds are singing and everything is wonderful. Then business slows down, but the bills keep coming in. You need to scramble to make more sales to pay your expenses. Profit is not guaranteed. You become laser-focused and worried about where the next client is coming from. Having corporate sponsors gives you an additional stream of revenue and frees you from the tyranny of focusing on acquiring clients.

SAY GOODBYE TO BOUNCED CHECKS AND DECLINED PAYMENTS

I love being a business owner and I'm a 20-year business veteran, but one of my least favorite parts of business is "chasing money." Don't you hate having to call customers to remind them to pay what they owe you? Me too. Collecting payments may have a negative effect on your relationship with the client who owes you money. That's why I encourage you to get the sponsor fee in one lump sum rather than installment payments. Since you're working with large companies, you don't need to deal with bounced checks and declined credit cards.

CREATE PROFITABLE, LIFE-CHANGING EVENTS

Here's one of the best-kept secrets: People invest their time and money to create amazing events, but many event producers only break even or worse, lose money. Many times the fee that attendees pay doesn't even cover the cost. When I hear these stories, it breaks my heart. Stop the madness!

With events, there are front-end revenues such as tuition, exhibitor fees, advertising, fundraising, product sales, and sponsorships. The back-end benefits include exposure for your property, clients, referrals, testimonials, media, and brand-building. Event producers rationalize that the back-end benefits will eventually cover their costs. While this may be somewhat true, I believe that people who put their hearts and souls into creating life-changing events should make a good profit with every event.

ADD CREATIVE FUNDING FOR YOUR DREAMS

Being an entrepreneur tends to lower your credit score because you make many purchases for your business through consumer credit. This makes it harder to get traditional financing, which is based on your consumer credit rating. With the credit markets being tight, there are all kinds of alternative funding solutions for business owners. Corporate sponsorship is a great creative funding strategy and you don't have to pay the money back. With corporate sponsor funding, you're not saddled with debt. There are no credit checks with corporate sponsor funding and I've even helped people in bankruptcy secure corporate sponsors.

HOW DO SPONSORSHIPS COMPARE WITH OTHER KINDS OF FUNDING?

JOINT VENTURES

A joint venture, or "affiliate relationship," is created when two people get together to sell a product or service and they split the profits from the sale. Joint ventures can be set up between someone with a large audience and someone who has a small database or no following. You get to build your audience and look behind the scenes at how to run a successful business. Joint ventures are a great way to build your audience and get some exposure. The advantage is that there is no start-up cost for a joint venture. The disadvantage is that you may need to pay a large commission to your joint venture partner.

LOANS

Small businesses and charities often have a hard time getting traditional funding. Commercial funding sources such as banks don't like to take risks on new and unproven businesses. Some business categories, such as restaurants and fashion, are considered too risky because of the intense competition and high failure rate. Also, getting institutional financing can be a frustrating and embarrassing experience. If you do manage to knock down the obstacles to traditional funding and secure a loan, you have now acquired debt. You need to pay back the loan with interest.

CREDIT CARDS

Many people use credit cards to start their businesses, events, non-profits and projects. You'll find many business owners have maxed out their credit cards because they believed strongly in what they were doing and were big risk-takers.

I've started businesses with credit cards because they provide quick but expensive money. However, sometimes the credit card company will flag you for charging too much and then lower your credit limit. They can also change your terms and raise your interest rate. Make sure that you use credit cards carefully as a short-term strategy to build your property.

GRANTS

Sponsorships are a marketing expense and grants are a donation. Grants are non-repayable funds disbursed by the grant maker (often a government department, corporation, foundation or trust), to a recipient, often, but not always, a non-profit entity, educational institution, business or individual.

In order to receive a grant, some form of grant application is usually required. Grant writing can be a tedious process and you'll need to fill out the grant submissions exactly according to the funder's specifications. Some people hire grant writers to navigate the waters and help them get grant funding.

Most grants are given to fund a specific project and require some level of compliance and reporting. The grant writing process involves an applicant submitting to a potential funder, either on the applicant's own initiative or in response to a request for a proposal from the funder. Sometimes grant makers require grant seekers to have some form of tax-exempt status, be a registered nonprofit organization, or a local government. A federal grant is an award of financial assistance from a federal agency to a recipient to carry out a public purpose of support or stimulation authorized by a law of the United States.

INVESTORS

You can get people to invest in your business. The advantages are funding, powerful partnerships, and quality introductions. However, you need to pay your investors back with interest or give them equity in your company.

Most people think investors are the holy grail of business, but sometimes they can be a nightmare. You start a business to have freedom and independence, but your investors can take this freedom away. They may become impatient, want changes to your business that you don't agree with, and get demanding. Sometimes it becomes like being in a bad marriage and you just want out. When dealing with investors, do your due diligence and check them out. Talk to other people who have worked with the investors and check personal references. With corporate sponsorships, you get to keep the control and ownership of your business.

Each of these funding methods has advantages and you can use them in combination with corporate sponsorships. In fact, when you approach a joint venture partner, bank, or investor for financing, let them know that you have corporate sponsorship. You'll immediately have more credibility. They'll know you are playing at a higher level and sometimes they'll give you the advantage on a silver platter!

WHAT SPONSORS GIVE YOU

WAYS TO START OVER FINANCIALLY WITH NO CREDIT CHECKS

Entrepreneurs typically have lower credit scores, at least for a while. It's almost a badge of honor. Sometimes new business owners have financial issues such as judgments, divorces, lawsuits and bankruptcies. With these on your file, you're considered "radioactive" in the traditional financing community. With corporate sponsorships, however, there are no credit checks. You don't need to show financials, bank statements or tax returns. In fact, I've helped many people with terrible credit and bankruptcies get sponsors. It's the perfect way to start over.

MEDIA AND PUBLIC RELATIONS OPPORTUNITIES

Would you like access to the top media and public relations minds? When you're featured in the media, it makes people trust you and they're more likely to do business with you. Media **coverage** amps up your credibility, so you should feature your media clips and other coverage on your web site, sponsor proposals, and marketing materials. The media help you get the word out about your company on a grand scale.

Corporate sponsors have access to public relations and marketing professionals you could only dream of hiring. When a corporate sponsor funds you, they have a stake in promoting you because it helps them. You'll often get access to their awesome public relations and media teams.

ONCE-IN-A-LIFETIME EXPERIENCES

You can get travel, clothing, advertising, contest giveaways, electronics, technology, and many other products and services free from your corporate sponsors. Right now, I'm looking at a beautiful all-in-one office printer that was provided by one of my sponsors.

You can also get once-in-a-lifetime experiences. I remember looking out from my beautiful room at the top of the Hyatt Grand Hotel after a sponsor had me flown to San Francisco. I saw the sunset over the Golden Gate Bridge. I heard the bells of the cable cars outside my room. My clients have done speaking and media tours in A-list cities, have met celebrities, and have been flown to exotic locations by their sponsors. They've been wined, dined, and treated like rock stars.

YOUR CHANCE TO PEEK BEHIND THE CURTAIN

Would you like an insight into how successful corporations with lots of money operate? Do you think you could apply some of their strategies to your business? Working with a corporate sponsor is your golden key to be an insider and learn how "big money" operates. You can be a fly on the wall and soak up their company culture like a sponge. It's the ultimate backstage pass to amazing business connections and success.

WHO QUALIFIES FOR CORPORATE SPONSORSHIPS?

SMALL BUSINESS OWNERS AND SOCIAL ENTREPRENEURS

Small business owners and social entrepreneurs make up a large component of my client base. I've helped lots of small business owners get funding from corporate sponsors. Social entrepreneurs want to change people's lives for the better, even create global change. This is conscious capitalism at its best. Being an entrepreneur gives you access to clients and prospects. You can build an audience and following for your business and then connect a corporate sponsor to that following. If you don't have an audience yet, don't worry. With collaborations, you can build your audience quickly.

EVENT PRODUCERS

Sponsors love events because there are many opportunities to connect with their core consumers. With events, you can provide sponsor benefits such as exhibitor opportunities, VIP privileges, contests, recognition from the platform, technological interaction, signage, sampling, peer and consumer engagement, couponing, even sales opportunities. Online events have value for sponsors. These include webinars, hangouts, videos, and other forms of online events and training. I encourage you to think about doing a live event because this is where sponsors can get some great connection opportunities and benefits. More connections equal more conversion. With events, sponsors can engage with your demographic in a positive light.

COACHES AND CONSULTANTS

These professionals work with clients for the long term and can keep the sponsor's name in front of their clients for the whole year, rather than just as a one-time event. The most successful coaches and consultants continually promote their businesses and they can include sponsors' names in their marketing and promotional campaigns.

SPEAKERS, AUTHORS, AND SELF-HELP EXPERTS

This group has a large fan base and they continually promote their books and brands. This makes them ideal for corporate sponsors. If you're a speaker, you don't necessarily need to put on your own event. For speakers, every time you do a presentation, it is considered a live event where you can include your sponsor.

At the Women's Small Business Expo, when speakers asked if they could bring their sponsor with them, I always said yes. If you're invited to speak on someone else's stage, ask the event producer if you can bring your sponsor or distribute the sponsor's marketing materials. They will usually say "yes" because they want the opportunity to meet and network with your corporate sponsor. For book authors, you can include sponsors in your book tour and place the sponsor's material in the physical books that are shipped to readers. As a self-help expert, you can give the sponsor exposure in your promotional campaigns. Don't forget online speaking, training, and campaigns. These are very viable promotional opportunities for your corporate sponsors.

ENTERTAINMENT

This includes music events, concerts, television, films, and even your child's theater group. Guy Laliberté was a street performer and started an innovative show called Cirque du Soleil. Guy is a gambler and an incredible risk-taker. When Cirque du Soleil came down from Canada to do its first show in California, they spent their entire budget and didn't even have enough money to get their performers back home after the shows. They had to sell tickets. There was no turning back. On a wing and a prayer, they performed to packed audiences and they made enough money to stay in business. As Cirque du Soleil grew, they added sponsors such as iShares, Infiniti, Xerox, SAP and MAC Cosmetics. The founder, Guy Laliberté, became a billionaire.

WEBSITES, BLOGGERS, APPS, AND MOBILE MARKETING

I've worked with clients who don't want to travel, speak, or do events. They want to run their web sites, publish their blogs, and create apps so they can do their business anywhere. You can also get sponsors for your online property. Just look at the popular social media sites. People open "free" accounts, but they are not entirely free. To join, you need to give the social media site information such as your age, education, and other juicy marketing information that companies love to know—and sometimes share. Their entire business model is based on advertising and sponsors.

MEDIA PERSONALITIES, WEB TV, RADIO, AND PODCASTS

We're not just running our businesses anymore. We're running media companies. Now many entrepreneurs host their own Web TV, radio shows and podcasts. Magazines now come in hard copy and online forms. All of these different new and traditional media are a perfect fit for corporate sponsors.

Podcasting is a powerful movement, where people broadcast a series of audio, video, PDF or ePub files through web syndication. Communications are accessed through a web feed and content can be pushed or accessed by the user. Podcasters are celebrated as experts and thought leaders by their audiences. I've had many clients come to me after hearing me as a featured guest on a podcast.

Internet radio involves streaming media, which can be enjoyed live or later as an archive file. It's also known as appointment radio, because listeners can hear content on their own time if they wish. These shows can be downloaded to an audio device and are portable. Some Internet radio shows are associated with terrestrial radio, which are traditional radio stations with call letters.

Web TV is video content that includes episodes produced for broadcast via the Internet. This makes it possible for people without deep pockets to become celebrities and experts without the barriers to entry that existed before.

SPORTS AND ATHLETES

Sports sponsorships are among the most established, visible, and lucrative forms of sponsorships. Just think of the last time you saw a sports event. The athletes may have worn sponsor logos on their apparel and accessories. The stadium had sponsor signage all through the venue. Athletes also get lucrative endorsement and sponsor deals.

Just think of NASCAR. You'll find sponsor logos on the cars, hats, food, beverages, in the center of the track, and even on TV when the drivers' stats appear. In researching NASCAR, sponsors found that people identified with the individual race car drivers, so drivers also get their own lucrative sponsor deals as individuals.

You may not have a sport as big as NASCAR, but maybe your child is involved in sports. Your child's sports team can be also be sponsored and many of the strategies that the big sports teams use can help your child in sports sponsorships.

NON-PROFIT CHARITIES

Non-profits give sponsors marketing benefits because people like to buy from companies that support worthy causes and give back to the community. Most savvy non-profits, such as Susan G. Komen, Habitat for Humanity and Make a Wish Foundation, have mastered the art of corporate sponsorship. In fact, there is often competition among organizations to sponsor certain popular causes. By sponsoring non-profit charities, sponsors can bask in the "halo effect" created by their charitable support, and everyone wins.

If you don't see your type of property on this list, don't worry. New types of properties are always being sponsored, so please feel free to contact me anytime.

WHY WOULD A COMPANY SPONSOR YOU?

> *"When we give cheerfully and accept gratefully, everyone is blessed."*
>
> **–Maya Angelou**

INCREASE BRAND LOYALTY

It's more expensive to recruit a new customer than to keep an existing customer. Sponsors pay big bucks to achieve brand loyalty among their existing customer base. Sponsors also like to think of ways to thank existing customers, such as loyalty programs that could include your property. Satisfied and loyal customers tell other people about their favorite brands and they need something to talk about. That's where you come in. Sponsoring properties and causes keeps the sponsor's brand fresh, makes it newsworthy, and lets the public know that they care about the community and their loyal customers.

Brand loyalty is extremely important now because of the proliferation of information and consumer choices. Sponsors need to work harder to ensure that people are loyal to their brands and even become brand cheerleaders. That's where your property can help them.

CREATE AWARENESS AND VISIBILITY

Sponsors need you to get the word out about their company and show their company in a positive light. If you endorse a brand, it creates more credibility than traditional media, where the public knows the company purchased its own advertising. The sponsor is borrowing your credibility and audience connection.

Some brands have extensive portfolios that include lesser-known divisions or products to promote. When Citibank sponsored me, the company had a lesser-known division, Women & Company, which did amazing work. Women & Company taught females about financial literacy so they could take charge of their economic futures, but not many people knew about this small division of Citibank. By sponsoring me, they had a connection to women business owners. We increased membership and gave visibility to Women & Company.

The second-tier sponsors need you to get the word out about their company. I recommend insurance companies as possible sponsors. Evolution Insurance, a wonderful brand, sponsored me. The company is an excess and surplus lines brokerage that provides options and solutions for specialty liability, professional, property, and casualty insurance. They wanted more women business owners to know about their brand and I was happy to promote them. Pursuing these kinds of second-tier sponsors can be a ripe opportunity for you.

CHANGE OR REINFORCE IMAGE

Some companies need a change to their public image. They may be older brands that want to become more relevant, or they may want to change public perception. Sponsorship puts a friendly face on the company. When FedEx sponsored me, the company wanted business owners to know that they were not an expensive, white-glove shipping company. In some categories, they were the economical choice for small and home-based businesses and they wanted to convey that message to entrepreneurs. Some companies may want to reinforce an image they've spent years and lots of money to create with the public and sponsorships are a great way to sustain image awareness.

DRIVE RETAIL TRAFFIC

You'll be extremely valuable to sponsors if you can help them **drive traffic to their brick-and-mortar and online retail stores.**

When Staples sponsored me, they provided coupons that drove traffic to their stores and their online retail site. You can help retail businesses by giving them exposure, publicity campaigns, contests, product reviews, product sampling, and couponing. If you have a retail store as a sponsor, you can also match them up to do cross-promotions with one of your other sponsors that wants to be featured by the retailer.

GROW THEIR CUSTOMER BASE

No matter how big a company is, they are always looking for more customers and clients. There is a natural attrition every year with businesses. Customers stop purchasing for many reasons, which including death, illness, buying from a competitor, and not needing the product or service anymore. The hunt for new customers is constant and all-consuming. Acquiring that coveted new customer is just the beginning. Then the romance begins. Each customer has a "lifetime value," which is based on a consumer's total purchases. Therefore, new and existing clients need to be nurtured.

OPEN UP A DESIRABLE GEOGRAPHIC TERRITORY

Some of my clients have received lucrative sponsor deals because the company saw opportunities in a certain geographic territory. One of my clients even had a sponsor tell her, "If you do an event in Las Vegas, we'll sponsor you." Be sure to ask prospective sponsors if they have plans to penetrate the area where you live, where you'll be speaking, or where your event will take place.

SHOWCASE COMMUNITY RESPONSIBILITY

People like to buy from companies that give back to the community and sponsorships showcase an organization's community commitment. It lets people know that the company is a good corporate citizen. Sponsorships also highlight the humanity of the company with stories from real people about how they love the brand. People buy emotionally and sponsor campaigns create an emotional connection with the brand. Most people don't have time to volunteer for their favorite charities, so "armchair philanthropy" is on the rise. People can help their communities and causes through companies they support.

ENTERTAIN CLIENTS

Why do you think companies pay a fortune to sponsor sports events and concerts? Because these are perfect opportunities to entertain clients. Sponsors can entertain clients in their private VIP boxes at sports stadium or fly them in for a once-in-a-lifetime concert. If you do events, you can offer sponsors hospitality privileges for their clients, such as private lounges, special hosts, preferred seating, meet-and-greets, autographed books, gift bags, etc. After the event, the sponsors' special clients can get thank you notes and a special gift. The list is endless.

RECRUIT AND RETAIN EMPLOYEES

Getting and keeping top employees is a prime directive of sponsors and they can use your property as an employee perk. Sponsors incentivize top performers by sending them to business conferences, sports events, entertainment, restaurants, and special events. Rewarding top salespeople is extremely important because, if they don't treat these income-producing employees well, they could move on to the competition.

Sponsors don't always want to create their own non-profits or events. They don't have people who can write books or deliver compelling speeches.

That's where you come in. You can inspire and reward key performers. These valuable employees get "can't-buy" experiences and your property could give team members something to strive for.

DIRECT CONNECTIONS WITH YOUR TARGET MARKET

Sponsors have initiatives to connect their brands with your target market, so tell sponsors more than you think they need to know. If your target market is growing or has purchasing power, then that makes you very attractive to sponsors. Think about creative ways for sponsor participation, where sponsors can engage with your target audience. Your target market is one of the biggest assets you have in the sponsor game, so be sure to do plenty of research and highlight that market's purchasing power, strengths, buying habits, and trends.

TO BE ON YOUR ADVISORY BOARD AND CONNECT WITH INFLUENTIAL THOUGHT LEADERS

Sponsors love to connect with people who are influential in business, politics, and the community. If you have connections or know someone who can connect you to these thought leaders, recruit them to be on your advisory board. Sponsors may want to support you for the opportunity to engage with key influencers.

One of the companies I know sponsored an author who also did speaking for people he met through the sponsor's advisory board. This was a constant source of opportunity for him that paid off, big time.

DEMONSTRATE CATEGORY LEADERSHIP

The top brands never rest on their laurels. They fight every day to stay there and maintain their category dominance. Coca Cola was a top brand in the U.S. and they spent lots of money to make their brand global, even when global wasn't cool. They constantly change their brand to add healthy options, keep it relevant, and do lots of image sponsorships. Coca-Cola has been a leader in the world of sponsorships since 1928.

OPPORTUNITY TO TEST A NEW PRODUCT OR SERVICE

Sampling and surveys are also benefits of corporate sponsorships. Companies can introduce new products, services, videos, testimonials, and product reviews through their corporate sponsorships. Dove started out as a soap invented by a dermatologist. Over the years, the brand was expanded to include products such as body lotion, hair care, body wash, and deodorant. For each new product, the company needed a marketing campaign that included sponsorships.

TO MAKE PEOPLE AWARE OF A LINE EXTENSION

Special K started out as a breakfast cereal that first hit the U.S. market in 1956. Now it's marketed as a low-fat product a person can eat to lose weight. Over the years, Kellogg's, Special K's parent company, expanded on the product's health and weight loss and created "The Special K Challenge," which says consumers can lose close to 10 pounds in two weeks by following the Special K diet. Kellogg's expanded the Special K line to include products such as shakes, snacks, and protein bars. To promote this line extension, they launched traditional advertising campaigns and sponsorships and now Special K is a lucrative part of the Kellogg's brand.

One of Special K's best commercials showed women stepping on a scale. Like many women, they were terrified to read the number. To their surprise, the scale gave them words of encouragement such as "You're an inspiration." Instead of punishing them for not being the perfect weight, they got verbal hugs.

DAMAGE CONTROL

This is a problem for your sponsors, but an opportunity for you. When you're seeking prospective sponsors, look for companies that are getting negative publicity and have a tarnished public image. These companies are ripe for corporate sponsorship.

I secured a major retailer as a sponsor because of negative publicity about how the company treated its female employees. It was even reported that the company paid women managers less than it paid men in the same jobs. When I talked to a company representative, I knew the organization was making positive changes and all the women I worked with there loved their employer. These women were well-paid power players and I was proud to promote them to women entrepreneurs. This company needed major damage control and sponsored me because I could show them in a positive light to women business owners with purchasing power.

IDENTIFICATION WITH A PARTICULAR LIFESTYLE

Image is important and sponsors want to be associated with certain lifestyles. There are certain "aspirational brands," such as luxury cars, apparel, beverages, hotels, and watches, that people *aspire* to own when they've finally "made it." These name brands become their trophies, manifestations of their hard work. Other brands want to identify with middle-market consumers to let people know that their products and services are affordable. Some brands want to identify with certain age groups and their buying cycles. By sponsoring you, these brands can be associated with lifestyles based on factors such as fun, youth, adventure, affluence, or family values.

ENHANCE COMMITMENT TO DIVERSITY AND ETHNIC GROUPS

If your property promotes diversity, tell sponsors about it. Diversity is an important issue in corporate America and many sponsors have initiatives for certain ethnic and societal groups that are gaining economic power. I've had sponsors tell me that if they don't succeed with the diversity markets, they won't survive as a company. That's powerful. Sponsors also look at the long view and know that years from now, the ethnic mix and buying power will change. They want to be part of this ethnic and cultural shift.

DRIVE SALES!

Did you notice the exclamation point? That's because most people forget that the goal of corporate sponsorships is to drive sales. Your sponsors need to get ROO and ROI. ROO is a return on objectives and ROI is a return on investment. Companies need to make sales so they can stay in business and remain competitive. Find out what their profit centers are. Some electronic companies have initiatives to make money on their insurance brands. Sponsors may not be looking for sales to spike right away, but you need to show sponsors how you're helping add to their bottom line. Show them how to follow the green so you can follow your dream.

> *"Obstacles are those frightful things you see when you take your eyes off your goal."*
>
> **—Henry Ford**

> ## SPONSOR SUCCESS STORY: STARS ON ICE
> ### Skating on Sponsored Ice
>
> In 1986, Olympic champion Scott Hamilton was shocked to learn that his contract with the Ice Capades was not renewed because show promoters thought male skaters wouldn't bring crowds of people into stadiums. He set out to prove them wrong. Hamilton, working with sponsors, promoters, and investors, created Stars on Ice, a show geared toward adults that featured Olympic skaters in group and solo performances. The production was first-rate, with lighting designers, sound engineers, and choreographers. The original tour went to only five cities and it ran on a shoestring.
>
> I suggested you should think about out-of-category sponsors. Stars on Ice could have approached an ice skate manufacturer as a sponsor to stay in their category, but they went for the big bucks. Stars on Ice sponsors have included Target, Discover Card, and Smuckers because these companies have the same family values. By the time it reached its tenth anniversary, Stars on Ice was reaching 55 cities in America alone.

WHAT SPONSORS WANT

Do you want to know how to crack the code and get sponsors? Here are some of the top things sponsors want from you.

TO KNOW THAT YOU UNDERSTAND THEIR GOALS

Sponsors want to know that you understand the company and its marketing campaigns, goals, and visions. You can learn this in your initial conversation with the sponsor, on the sponsor's web site, by reading articles, social media, and by doing an Internet search. If your prospective sponsor is a public company, you can order the annual report. When you talk to the sponsor, remember to ask them about their goals first, then go into your presentation and tell them how you can help them accomplish their goals.

DEMOGRAPHICS

Your target demographic (also called your target market) is one of the most valuable assets you can offer a sponsor. There are various ways to research your demographic. You can do an Internet search for statistics on your target demographic. Your demographic reads certain publications. You can order the media kit for these publications and get some great statistics for your sponsor proposal. You can pay a market research firm or check local colleges to see if they have research available.

PLATFORM

Sponsors want to know you have extended reach to people who buy things (think Oprah). These could be your clients, people on your email list, your company database, your advisory board, and your strategic alliances. Remember, if you don't have an audience yet, other people do. Use the powerful strategies of borrowed credibility, collaborations, media, and joint ventures.

CAUSE-RELATED MARKETING OPPORTUNITIES

Cause-related marketing is a sales or promotional partnership between the sponsor and a property helping the community or a special "cause" for good. People buy more from companies that give back to the community, so the sponsor wants to be known as a good corporate citizen. By aligning their brand with the life-changing work you do, sponsors can bask in the "halo effect."

COMPELLING SPONSOR PROPOSAL

If you want top-tier sponsors, you need a sponsor proposal. It's also called the sponsorship deck, or prospectus. This is a business plan and snapshot of your property's benefits. The sponsor proposal contains the story of your property, mission statement, sponsor benefits, demographics, marketing plan, goals, media opportunities, advisory board, and sponsor fees. The sponsor proposal is the most important, but least understood, document in the sponsor industry. To be successful, the proposal needs the correct language and it needs to be compelling.

DELIVERABLES

You need clarity and focus in your sponsor proposal. Vagueness just won't make it. Here's an example of showing your sponsor deliverables. Rather than telling the sponsor they will get media exposure, let them know that one of your media sponsors is the Hometown Business Journal, which has a circulation of more than 60,000 people who make more than $100,000 a year.

VALUE

Your sponsorship offering needs to be more than a win-win proposition. The benefits need to be so compelling that working with you is an easy decision. The mistake many people make is to calculate their expenses, then ask for that amount of money from a sponsor. Sponsorship is a value-based proposition. It's not based on your expenses.

INTEGRITY

Sponsors want to know that you have integrity and credibility. They will test you to see if you do what you say. Get them their information on time and arrive early for appointments. If you can't get requested information to them on time, let them know that you're working on it so they won't think you've forgotten about them. Give them regular reports and updates. Keep in mind that you need to pass their unspoken tests. They want to see if you have integrity and can handle their brand image.

EXPERIENCE

Sponsors want experience, but don't worry. If you don't have it, someone else does. Tell the sponsor about your previous experience in a related business. Surround yourself with key influencers on your advisory board. Tell the sponsor about leading-edge companies you know or have worked with. If you have a new property, have a long-term marketing plan.

RIGHT OF FIRST REFUSAL

The right of first refusal (ROFR) is a contractual right that grants a sponsor the right to match any sponsorship offer your property receives during a specific period in the sponsor's defined product category. It usually gives the sponsor the right to match the terms of any deal your property negotiates in the renewal process.

It's important to be clear about when your sponsor deal begins and ends. Be specific about how the renewal/ ROFR process works. Provide as much detail as possible about these provisions and walk through various scenarios of how the process will work when it's time to renew or comply with the terms of the right of first refusal.

FOLLOW-UP

Follow-up can make or break you in the sponsor game. I've seen many people miss out on lucrative sponsor deals because they lacked follow-up skills. When talking with a prospective sponsor, always make a follow-up appointment. Confirm the appointment by email. Make a follow-up plan and always know your next step. If you're not strong in follow-up, find someone who is.

TO AVOID RISK

Remember, dealing with sponsors is different from working with entrepreneurs. While entrepreneurs are risk-takers, sponsors want to avoid risk. They need to be sure you're not going to embarrass them in a cloud of scandal. They need to know that you're with them for the long haul and your message won't provoke a backlash.

When you start talking with a potential sponsor, remember that you're dealing with a human being who needs to balance the interests of superiors, colleagues, and customers. These people need to make sure their company doesn't deviate too far from its present course. It's best to promote teamwork and create rapport in your conversations. Be sure your pitch is different enough for them to sponsor you, but not too different from what they've already done.

LEAD TIME

Lastly, let's talk about lead time. As entrepreneurs, we can think of a new idea and put it into practice quickly, but the timetable is quite different with corporate America. Your sponsor needs to follow company procedures. Ideas may need to go through meetings, reports, and teams before they can get sponsorships approved. The more lead time you offer, the more successful you'll be with your corporate sponsors.

"Teaching kids sound financial habits at an early age gives all kids the opportunity to be successful when they are an adult."

— Warren Buffett

SPONSOR SUCCESS STORY: JUNIOR ACHIEVEMENT

Sponsoring Youth to Build Businesses

In 1919, Horace Moses, Theodore Vail, and Senator Murray Crane founded Junior Achievement (JA) as a collection of after-school business clubs for students in Springfield, Massachusetts. Students learned how to think and plan for business and acquire supplies. They learned to build their own products, advertise, sell, and even how to read financial reports. Before long, JA students were competing in regional expositions and trade fairs and rubbing elbows with top business leaders.

Today, Junior Achievement concentrates on financial literacy, work readiness, and entrepreneurship. With the generous support of sponsors, donors, and more than 112,000 volunteers, Junior Achievement reaches approximately four million students per year.

One of the highlights of my career was serving as a judge at the Competitive Edge contest, where students created and presented their working businesses. They shared their business plans, which included cost of goods, profit potential, marketing, even social responsibility, which is how their businesses will help the world.

Junior Achievement sponsorship opportunities included a bowl-a-thon, golf tournament, and adopt-a-classroom. These opportunities were included in their sponsor proposals. Sponsors of Junior Achievement have included Citibank, Sport Chalet, Toyota, Bank of America, H&R Block, and One West Bank.

GETTING SPONSOR-READY

"Surround yourself with only people who are going to lift you higher."

–Oprah Winfrey

CREATE YOUR SUCCESS TEAM

One of the best ways to accelerate your goal achievement is through a Success Team. The concept of the success team is based on the mastermind alliance, described by Napoleon Hill in his groundbreaking book, *Think and Grow Rich*. The success team is a collection of people (minds) gathered in perfect harmony for a definite purpose. Having more than one mind working on a topic creates an invisible energy in a think-tank environment, which opens up new insights for members. Being with successful people who have confidence in you and are actively working on behalf of your success instills more confidence and initiative.

Surrounding yourself with those who balance out your strengths, weaknesses, experience, and expertise helps widen your horizons as you gain a different perspective on issues. The best success teams develop strong relationships and increase self-esteem and personal power.

A success team brings out the human potential in its members. Marriage and business partnerships are the ultimate success teams. With a great and supportive partner, you can accomplish more than you would using just the power of one mind. Synergy is created when the whole is greater than the sum of its parts. When you experience breakthroughs, your group is working at a synergy level.

Your success team will be **made up** of the people who support you and hold your visions in light. You'll need different kinds of people on your success team.

TYPES OF SUCCESS TEAMS

I've expanded the concept of the mastermind into a cadre of different teams for different purposes: The "you-can-do-it" team, family team, professional team, investor team, and mentor team.

You-Can-Do-It Team. This is a group of friends and associates who believe in you and push you to achieve excellence. This includes the business associate you call with company problems and a friend you meet with for margaritas and guacamole. These are your special cheerleaders. They believe in you and hold your dreams in the light. They have a special talent for motivation. When you want to quit, these extraordinary individuals urge you to raise the bar for yourself and not settle for the ordinary. Sometimes they know you even better than you know yourself. The structure for "You-Can-Do-It" team meetings is informal and casual, usually consisting of telephone calls, online communications, in between daily tasks and meeting for dinners. Don Foster Gutridge tells a story of a man named Bob who caught wind of a rumor that his company was going to let him go. Because of the encouragement of his You-Can-Do-It Team, Bob turned the situation around, bought the company, sold it, and then retired, extremely wealthy.

Family Team. Your marriage, primary relationship, and family are the ultimate success teams. The interactions of the family success teams are intense, relaxed and heart-warming.

Iris Rainer Dart called her cousin Sandy when anything important happened in her life: a new job, her boyfriend proposing, the birth of her son, etc. Iris and Sandy went through school, boyfriends, jobs, parenting, and life. The cousins shared all of their triumphs and tribulations. If you hurt one of the women, the other came to her defense. Inspired by her marvelous success team with her cousin Sandy, Iris wrote a book about two women who become lifetime friends. She created the memorable characters C.C. Bloom and Hillary Whitney in her poignant novel *Beaches,* later made into a major motion picture.

Professional Team. These are paid professionals who help you with your success. They include accountants, lawyers, insurance agents, sponsor experts, consultants, and coaches. For this success team, you need to take out your wallet and invest in your success. Professional advisors don't cost you money, they *save* you money. A sponsor expert will help you create a winning proposal and advise you about which sponsors to approach or avoid. Accountants help you with your financials and tax advice. Attorneys help you set up your non-profit or business with the correct legal structure. Insurance is essential to your wealth-building and you need coaches, consultants, and mentors for great brainstorming and guidance. The structure of a professional team meeting is formal. Time is definitely money here.

Investor Team. This includes people who help fund you, including bankers, financial institutions, non-traditional financers, grantors, individual investors, donors, and sponsors. Most people want to project an image of a strong company and are hesitant to go to their investor team for advice, but this is a mistake. These are people experienced in business and non-profits. Their advice is invaluable. Since they have "skin in the game," they have a vested interest in your success.

Mentor Team. These visionaries play at a higher level than you are at right now. They are where you aspire to be. These luminaries may also possess skills and knowledge that you want to tap into. The advisory board is the classic mentor team.

Jack Canfield, co-author of the *Chicken Soup for the Soul* books, recounts a story of a man who was highly successful by society's standards. He was making a million dollars a year. But even someone at this level had aspirations. He wanted to produce even more income, so he formed an alliance with individuals who were making at least five million dollars a year.

BE CLEAR ABOUT YOUR PROPERTY

If you don't have clarity about your property, you'll create confusion with your potential sponsors and the confused mind says no. If you're doing an event, tell the sponsor the date, location, and venue. Define what will happen each day and the great takeaways the attendees will receive. If you have a business, project or cause, know all the demographics and the sponsor benefits. Give the sponsor activation ideas, which is how they will engage with your target market. Since sponsorships are customized, think of things your sponsor can "own."

UPLEVEL YOUR WEB SITE AND ONLINE PRESENCE

Your prospective sponsors will check out your web site, so make sure it looks professional. The best web sites mix credibility and personality. You want to project credibility, but not look like everyone else. You can upgrade your web site rather quickly and you don't need to spend lots of money. Just look at some web sites that you like and that have been successful at getting sponsors.

Make sure your web site is easy to navigate and have someone re-check for spelling. I'm always surprised at how many typos I see on the Internet. The fonts and layout should be consistent for a professional look. For a clean web site, a white background is best. The most important pages are

- home page
- about us page

- FAQ page
- media info
- contact us

MAKE IT EASY FOR THE SPONSOR TO CONTACT YOU

If your "contact us" page includes a form people need to fill out to contact you, remove it immediately! Sponsors and media will *not* take the time to fill these out. Instead, they will move on to someone they can contact directly. Make it easy for the prospective sponsor to contact you from your web site by listing all of your contact information, including physical address, phone number, social media links, and email address. You can even put your phone number on the top header of each page.

BE SURE YOUR ONLINE BRANDING IS CONSISTENT

Make frequent checks of your blog, because sponsors will pay you for blog posts that promote their brand. Your social media should also have the same brand identity as your web site. Make sure there is nothing embarrassing on your social media in photos, groups, and postings.

MAKE SURE YOUR OFFLINE MARKETING MATERIALS BRAND YOU CORRECTLY

Your other marketing materials, such as business cards, company brochure, direct mail pieces, flyers, program books, etc., should be printed with clean graphics on good paper stock. Make sure your logo and visual branding are consistent and use a professional graphic designer. I got WalMart, Bank of America, and IBM as my first sponsors because I invested in a sponsor proposal with compelling benefits and first-rate graphics. Then I made sure that my online and offline brand identities were consistent. It gives sponsors a level of comfort when they see your business card, then go to your web site and see that they're in the right place.

BUILD YOUR AUDIENCE

When you go to events, exhibit, or speak in public, have a lead-collection device. At one time, I just collected business cards. Then I realized that people ran out of cards, or didn't even take their cards to a business meeting. Now when I speak, I pass out a raffle prize drawing form and ask them if they want to be included on my email list. Make it easy to unsubscribe if they don't want to be included in your email marketing. Make your web site a super-powered list-building machine that works for you 24/7. Encourage people to opt in and give you their contact information when they come to your web site by offering them an incentive such as a free special report, audio training, videos, or a book.

GET FEATURED IN THE MEDIA

The media are out there looking for great stories like yours. Write a press release about your business or cause and include some human interest in the story. People like to know about the business founders and what sparked their passion.

When doing media interviews, use the classic "dip" formula. Explain where you are now and how you overcame obstacles to your success. When people see that you've experienced hard times, they can relate to you as a real person. Don't be overly concerned with impressing people. Be vulnerable and let your humanity shine. Also, learn to talk in short sentences, or "sound bites," when doing interviews. There should be a good volley between you and the interviewer and you shouldn't monopolize the conversation.

Some media are friendlier to promotion than others are. Radio is like a flea circus that happily promotes you as a guest. If you're doing a radio interview, ask the host if you can give something away to the listeners. Then you can tell listeners to go to your web site where they can sign up for your "need to know information." Large television outlets with morning shows are consumer-focused and usually won't let you give out your contact information. Get to know the policy of the specific medium before your appearance.

Online media sometimes let you include a link to your web site or a resource box. The resource box is a short bio about you with the web site link. The link doesn't always need to go to the home page of your web site. It can go to a special landing page where people can opt in and give you their contact information. You can also use certain web codes to test the results of your marketing and media.

START NETWORKING WITH PEOPLE IN CORPORATE AMERICA

Ask the people you know for introductions to the key influencers. Go to events where business and marketing professionals hang out. Don't network with the person. Go for their Rolodex. If they can't help you, they may know someone who can. In "How to Sell Anything to Anybody," author Joe Girard put forth the concept of "The Law of 250." This concept is that most people know about 250 people who'd show up at their funeral or wedding. When you take this a step further, you realize the tremendous opportunity in The Law of 250 – each of your 250 contacts knows an additional 250 people for you to meet. Get busy and start cultivating these contacts.

GET TRAINING ABOUT CORPORATE SPONSORSHIPS

This book is only the start of your training for getting corporate sponsors. The risks and rewards are great, so it's worth investing in your training, especially learning how to create an industry-standard sponsor proposal. Make sure that whoever gives you advice about sponsorship knows about sponsor proposals, marketing, **and** outreach, and has experience in getting corporate sponsors. My company provides training and consultation about corporate sponsors, so please feel free to contact me at www.SponsorConcierge.com.

START LOOKING FOR A CHARITABLE PARTNER

You may have a charity that's close to your heart. If not, start your search for a charitable partner so you can offer sponsors the benefits of cause-related marketing, where they will be perceived as a good corporate citizen by giving back to the community.

One of the most important factors about your charitable partner is the relationship between you and your charity. When many of my clients try to approach established charities, they don't even get a return phone call or email. This tells you that the non-profit is definitely not a match for you. There should be synergy between you and your non-profit. You promote them and they promote you. It may be better to collaborate with a smaller, emerging charity where you can form a rapport with them.

Your charitable partner should also be a logical fit with your property. I've always loved animals and can't even imagine my life without a pet. I'm the original crazy cat lady and have always taken in rescue animals. When I first started Women's Small Business Expo, I wanted to have an animal rescue group as my charitable partner, but it was not a logical match with women's entrepreneurship. My charitable partner became Junior Achievement, which teaches boys and girls about entrepreneurship, because this relates to my property.

Finally, be sure to choose just one charitable partner. If you promote too many causes, it dilutes the message. Even though I don't spotlight animal rescue as my charitable property, I still donate privately to animal organizations.

DON'T MAKE BIG DEMANDS OF YOUR CHARITABLE PARTNER

Exposure and donations motivate charitable partners. If you can give your charity some exposure, provide fundraising opportunities, and help them with donations, they will promote you in return.

Non-profits need to comply with some stringent guidelines and practices. Their boards often make decisions. Charities are very protective of their image and reputation, so don't assume that you will be featured on their web site or their campaigns.

Wait until you have worked with the charity before you ask for big favors. Even though he didn't have a relationship with the non-profit, one of my clients asked a very well-known charity if he could be featured on their web site and they told him that it would cost him a small fortune.

MAKE A SPONSOR WISH LIST

Getting sponsors starts with a thought and a vision. Let's begin right now and make your Sponsor Wish List, companies that you would like to sponsor you. What most people do is write down a few top-tier companies and try to pursue them. Other people start by pursuing their "love brands," the companies they use all the time. This is a recipe for frustration because sponsorship is a numbers game.

Don't fall in love with just a few brands on your Sponsor Wish List and fantasize about how you will spend the sponsor fees they give you. Instead, make a Sponsor Wish List of prospective companies that includes both top-tier and second-tier sponsors. This will make you more successful in your sponsor outreach. Also, be willing to go beyond your industry for sponsors.

TOP-TIER SPONSORS

These are top-of-mind brands that come to mind immediately because they spend lots of money on advertising. They are usually mature brands with lots of employees and big infrastructures. Top-tier companies have healthy budgets for sponsorships and a process in place for submitting your property for funding.

I love the banking category. I have worked with many banking sponsors, so we'll use this as an example. Think of a few banks and write them down now. Chances are, these are the top-tier banks in the industry. Next, write down some other top-tier sponsors in other categories.

TOP-TIER SPONSORS LIST

_____
_____
_____
_____
_____

SECOND-TIER SPONSORS

Now let's go a bit deeper and list the second-tier banks. These could be smaller financial institutions and local community banks. You can find them easily on the Internet. Then write down some more second-tier sponsors in other categories.

SECOND-TIER SPONSORS LIST

_____
_____
_____
_____
_____

Second-tier companies are wonderful to work with because the decision makers are much more accessible. They also need you more because they don't have the brand awareness of their larger competitors. And they have money. Their budgets are healthy and you can help them gain market share and promote their brand.

With top-tier companies, you usually have the Fortune 500. With the addition of the second tier, you could have access to thousands of companies and your chances of success in the sponsor world increase exponentially.

LOVE BRANDS

Many of my clients want to approach brands they already use and recommend. They use a specific shampoo, shipping company, bank, car, food, computer, etc., and feel these companies would be great sponsors because they are already product evangelists.

LOVE BRANDS LIST

_____
_____
_____
_____
_____

You may love a company, but don't expect it to love you back. The people in the sponsorship departments are probably disconnected from you, so your cheerleading may not carry much weight. In addition, a pet peeve of sponsors is people who come to them with a sense of entitlement, expecting sponsorship because they use the company's product or service. Approach your love brands with an attitude of gratitude and you'll create great energy and love.

OUT-OF-CATEGORY SPONSORS

For more success with corporate sponsors, go out of your category. Let's say you're doing a live event for mothers. It's natural to want to approach companies that produce toys, children's clothing, etc. But think about the lives of today's mothers. They get up in the morning, wash their hair, brush their teeth, use their computers, get in their cars, drive to the bank, plan vacations for their families, etc. You can approach these (and other) out-of-category sponsors: shampoo, toothpaste, computers, automotive, banking, and travel. By expanding the categories of companies for corporate sponsorship, you'll create more funding opportunities.

OUT-OF-CATEGORY SPONSORS LIST

_____
_____
_____
_____
_____

Success Team Members and People Who Could Make Introductions

_____
_____
_____
_____
_____

Service Providers, Utility Companies, and People Recently Paid

_____
_____
_____
_____
_____

Products and Services Used by Your Target Market

_____
_____
_____
_____
_____
_____
_____

You can also go to www.SponsorConcierge.com to fill out your Wish List and Sponsor Action Plan.

SPONSOR SUCCESS STORY: MOVEMBER

A Hairy Cause

It all started with a bunch of Australian mates sitting around a barbeque with beer. The guys said everything eventually comes back into fashion. They wanted to see if they could make mustaches cool again. They started growing mustaches and getting comments from co-workers, friends, and family. Soon people began to ask if these dudes were growing their mustaches for a charity.

They did some research and found out that men's cancer charities get only a small percentage of money compared to women's cancer organizations. They decided to grow mustaches in November for awareness of men's testicular cancer and called it "Movember." Men grow mustaches, register with Movember, and ask friends and family for donations. Some men even come to their Thanksgiving dinners and find out that their grandfathers had testicular cancer. It motivates them to get early detection for cancer prevention.

Mo Bros, as well as Mo Sistas, participate. Movember has become a global movement, inspiring more than 3 million men and women in 21 countries. More than 1.1 million Mo Bros and Mo Sistas around the world have joined the movement and have raised more than $147 million for men's cancer awareness, research, and prevention.

Sponsors have included Wheaties, Tom's Shoes, Art of Shaving, 7 for all Mankind, and Gillette.

MYTHS ABOUT SPONSORSHIP

> *"You must understand that seeing is believing, but also know that believing is seeing."*
>
> **— Denis Waitley**

I NEED TO BE A NON-PROFIT.

I've always been a for-profit business. Many of my clients have received sponsor funding for their for-profit businesses. Capitalism is not a dirty word in sponsorships. In fact, sponsors understand that you need profit and revenues. Think of the many for-profit sponsorships in the world of sports, events, music, theatre, conferences, online, and media.

I NEED TO BE IN SPORTS.

Sports sponsorships are the most visible area of sponsorships. To get sponsorships, you don't need to be an athlete or represent a sports team. You can be a business owner, speaker, author, event producer, entrepreneur, media personality, consultant, or charity and get sponsorships. Just look around and you'll see all kinds of examples.

I created my company, Sponsor Concierge, because there were plenty of companies in sports sponsorships, but not many people helping charities and businesses. I love helping entrepreneurs and causes fund their dreams and I've never looked back.

THIS IS TOO SOPHISTICATED FOR ME.

Others perceive sponsorships as sophisticated or just out of their reach and this is actually an advantage for you. Their lack of confidence and false perceptions weed out your competition. They don't try to get corporate sponsors, but *you* will. According to marketing expert Dan Kennedy, there is beauty in things that seem complicated. If something were easy, then everyone would do it.

MY BUSINESS IS TOO SMALL.

Remember, I started getting sponsors when I was just a kitchen-table business. In fact, I shared the kitchen table with my cat, so you couldn't get any smaller than I was. I was a one-person micro-business with no audience or experience. Clients, mentors, events and sponsors helped me grow my business. I didn't wait until everything was perfect. Instead, I used sponsors to help me grow.

I DON'T HAVE ENOUGH EXPERIENCE.

Look at some successful properties that have great corporate sponsors and read their stories. You'll see that everyone needed to start somewhere and they probably had humble beginnings. You can get sponsors, even if you're just starting out, with great collaborations, a long-term plan, and a great sponsor proposal.

I'M INDEPENDENT. I DON'T WANT SPONSORS TO INFLUENCE ME.

Entrepreneurs are rugged individualists and they don't want anyone to put restrictions on their businesses. They fear that corporate sponsors will influence their content and they will become corporate slaves. None of my clients has ever had a sponsor try to change their core values or content. The sponsor gives you a cash or in-kind fee and they want *you* to do the work. This is great news, because the beauty of corporate sponsorship is that you design the program. If the sponsor suggests something and you're not comfortable with it, then just tell them it's not part of the sponsorship program.

I'M NOT READY YET.

Don't worry if everything isn't in place with your business. Web sites are never finished. You'll never have your perfect elevator speech and you can get the appropriate legal or non-profit status while applying for sponsorship.

Perfectionism is a trap that keeps people from moving forward. Take it from a recovering perfectionist: I've sent out sponsor letters with typos, had web sites that were very embarrassing, and said the wrong things to prospective sponsors. I made mistakes and learned lessons. In fact, there's no better way to learn than experience, so get your feet wet and start making mistakes.

BIGGEST MISTAKES PEOPLE MAKE

> *"Isn't it nice to think that tomorrow is a new day with no mistakes in it yet?"*
>
> **— L.M. Montgomery**

I'm the living embodiment of Murphy's Law. In fact, I've made every mistake in getting sponsors. Trial and error is expensive, so here are the biggest and most common mistakes people make.

NOT ASKING FOR ENOUGH MONEY

Unbelievably, asking for a small amount of money can work against you. Ask for enough money, so the prospective sponsor will take you seriously. You can't ask for a small amount of money to get your foot in the door and then radically increase your sponsor fee. Sponsorship doesn't work that way.

Remember, companies are downsizing. This means they are putting increased pressure on their employees' time. If you don't ask for enough money, the people who handle sponsorships may think it's not worth their time. Establish your worth at the beginning. It takes as much work to get pennies as it does to get dollars, so why not ask for the big bucks?

PUTTING THE WRONG BENEFITS IN THE SPONSOR PROPOSAL

You need specific compelling benefits in your sponsor proposals, or you'll be rejected and you won't even know why. The first thing people think about is putting the sponsor's logo on their web site. This is actually a low-level benefit because the sponsor probably already has brand name recognition. It also telegraphs to the prospective sponsor that you may lack experience and professionalism.

MAKING IT ALL ABOUT YOU

Most people wax rhapsodic about their property because it's what they know and can talk about. *Sponsorship is not about you.* It's about your prospective sponsor. I love storytelling in the sponsor proposal because it makes you memorable, creates an emotional connection, and spotlights your humanity. However, you need to connect your personal story and the description of your property to your sponsor benefits. Talk about how you will add value to your sponsor.

BIG FILE ATTACHMENTS

You can email your sponsor proposals and quick facts sheets as attachments, but watch the file size. Sponsors don't want to open large attachments because they think such files could pose a threat to their security, or take too long to open. If you convert your files to Adobe PDF format, this will decrease the file size. If the file is still too large (above 10MB), then you can have a graphic artist reduce the file size without reducing the quality of the document. You can also put the sponsor proposal on a web page the prospective sponsor can link to.

UNPROFESSIONAL PHONE ETIQUETTE

"The telephone is a good way to talk to people without having to offer them a drink."

— Fran Lebowitz

When you first talk to your corporate sponsors, they may only know you (and form a perception of you) based on what they hear on the phone. Therefore, you must think of your phone calls as auditions for success.

Use a good-quality phone line. I like to use a landline or Internet phone such as Skype. If you're on a cell phone, make sure the line is clear and that the call won't get dropped. You never get a second chance to make that all-important first impression. Disable call waiting and if you have a multi-line phone, put the ringer for the other phones on silent.

Sponsor seekers call me and when I call them back, they answer, "Hello." Ugh! They even make me hold while they get a pen to write. Can you believe it? Sometimes there are loud children and pets in the background. How unprofessional. This will turn off sponsors because it erodes your credibility. How can they trust you to represent their brand image when you can't even represent yourself correctly on the phone?

Your phone voice should be a bit slower than your normal tone. People tend to talk faster on the phone, especially when leaving voicemail, but a slow and measured voice is more professional. Practice enunciating and when you leave a phone number, remember to use correct pauses.

Always answer your phone professionally and include your business name. I know you can't control it completely, but if you're working from home try to keep sounds from children and pets to a minimum.

FORGETTING THAT INTEGRITY IS PART OF YOUR BRAND

Always do what you say. Your word is your bond. Show up on time or early for in-person and phone meetings. Sponsors judge you based on your integrity, so never fake an answer to a question. This destroys your credibility and it may destroy your relationship with the sponsor. If a sponsor asks you something you don't know, simply say you'll get back to them with the answer. This gives you a great opportunity to do some follow-up and create a trust relationship.

POOR FOLLOW-UP

> *"Those people blessed with the most talent don't necessarily outperform everyone else. It's the people with follow-through who excel."*
>
> **— Mary Kay Ash**

"Three Feet from Gold: Turn Your Obstacles into Opportunities," by Sharon Lechter and Greg Reid (in the "Think and Grow Rich" series), informs us that many people give up when they are only "three feet from gold" because of poor follow-up skills. In sponsorships, your fortune is in your follow-up. Be pleasantly persistent. Follow-up establishes trust in your sponsor relationship and companies appreciate your checking in with them.

Sponsors have told me they don't mind follow-up as long as you're giving them new information and not the same old robo-calls and robo-emails.

NOT HAVING AN INDUSTRY-STANDARD SPONSOR PROPOSAL

The sponsor proposal is the most important, but least understood, document in the sponsor world. Without it, don't even bother to approach sponsors. If you're going after the big bucks, you'll need an industry-standard sponsor proposal with appropriate compelling benefits. Teams and committees make sponsor decisions, usually after you're long gone, so the sponsor proposal needs to do the heavy lifting and sell for you.

CORPORATE SPONSORSHIP IS NOT FREE MONEY OR GET RICH QUICK

Yes, it's true that you don't need to pay the money back, but you need to provide quality, value, and service to your corporate sponsor. Sponsoring you is a marketing expense for them and your sponsor expects you to provide marketing and promotion for them, instilling them with both tangible and intangible benefits, such as the goodwill you will create for their brand.

WHERE TO FIND SPONSORS

"The way to get started is to quit talking and begin doing."

—Walt Disney

INTERNET

Find out what similar properties are doing and check out who's sponsoring them. Organizations that have sponsored something similar to what you're doing are more likely to sponsor you. For instance, if you're doing a college tour, find out which companies are targeting the college and youth markets. People frequently ask me what happens when sponsors are funding something similar to what you're doing. Will their budgets dry up? Don't worry. Just because they sponsor other properties, it doesn't mean they'll run out of money.

If you approach sponsors who work with properties similar to yours, you don't need to educate them about the value of your demographics. They already know that, so others have already done part of the selling process for you.

TRADE SHOWS

Go to trade shows and talk to exhibitors who represent companies that could be your sponsors. Stop by their booths when there's not much traffic, so they'll have more time to talk with you. The key influencer, who can greenlight a sponsorship, probably won't be there, so talk to the person at the booth. What you can do is ask the person at the trade show booth for contact information for the person in the marketing department at the company. When you call the prospective sponsor, say that the person at the exhibitor booth referred you. This is a quality introduction and turns a cold lead into a warm introduction.

EVENTS

At networking events, let people know you're looking for sponsors. Charitable events are also fertile ground for sponsors because you'll meet the movers and shakers at these events and on their non-profit boards. You can even speak at their charity events. You won't get paid, but it can be a great conduit to clients, media, sponsors, and more speaking opportunities. You'll be surprised at how many people can refer you to the decision makers in sponsor companies. After they give you some leads, thank them and ask if you can do anything for them.

ANYONE INTERESTED IN YOUR PROPERTY

Start a list of people who are interested in what you do. They could be prospects, attendees, vendors, donors, and customers. They know you, have a relationship with your property and understand what you do. This is a natural place to look for sponsors. Most people go outside of their proprietary database when they look for sponsors, but this is a great place to start.

MEDIA CAMPAIGNS

Pay attention to companies that are doing media campaigns. If you see an established company or new brand running an aggressive marketing campaign, it means they are spending lots of money to educate people about their brand. This could be a great prospective sponsor for you. Listen to the radio, watch television, look at billboards, and check out online advertising with an eye for possible sponsors.

DIRECTORIES

There are listings of companies who have sponsored properties. These companies are cold leads that need to be worked. Make sure you, or whoever contacts these companies, have good phone etiquette and sales training. Also, ask how often the lists are updated. The speed of business is so fast now that older lists may give marginal results.

SOCIAL MEDIA

Social media sites are good for researching who the key influencers are in the company and for starting discussions. Sometimes you can send messages to the decision makers through social media, rather than traditional email, and get better results. You can follow companies and get the latest news on their product launches and upcoming campaigns.

Query your social media following to see if any of them know someone at a specific company on your Sponsor Wish List or do a general request to your following to see if they know of any companies that might sponsor you.

YOUR CLIENTS AND PROSPECTS

Work the phone. Ask your current customers, clients, and prospects if they will sponsor you or if they know anyone who might be interested in the opportunity. You can also ask your family, friends, and your success teams if they can make some introductions on your behalf.

RESEARCH TO STRENGTHEN YOUR SPONSOR OFFERING

*"Research is formalized curiosity.
It is poking and prying with a purpose."*

—Zora Neale Hurston

Here are some great ways to research your demographics:

INTERNET

Do searches on the demographics by typing "statistics, purchasing, purchases, buying power, etc." Then add your demographic. If this information is not available, find out how many people are in your demographic. Then find out their annual household incomes. When you multiply the two numbers, you get their annual buying power.

MEDIA KIT

You can contact publications that your demographic reads and request a media kit. The media kit will tell you amazing things about your target market. I've seen media kits that talk about how often people buy new cars and computers.

UNIVERSITIES

Sometimes universities and colleges have research departments that can give you current research on the buying habits, age range, gender mix, income, etc., of your demographics.

HIRE A MARKET RESEARCH FIRM

You may want to hire a market research firm and work with their professional staff to gather data and psychographics about your target audience.

ASSOCIATIONS

With so many community, civic, and professional associations, there's a good chance you'll find an association that's perfect for you and your target market. These associations do periodic surveys of their membership and can give you beautiful research.

YOUR SURVEYS

Now there are online tools for you to do your own surveys. This could be valuable information if you've built up a great audience. When doing a survey, you need to give the respondents an incentive, such as getting a free private consultation from you or making them eligible for a prize drawing.

SPONSORS PAY YOU FOR DEMOGRAPHICS

Remember, sponsors pay you to connect them to people who buy things, so they want to know the type of people you are connecting them to.

Here are some things sponsors want to know about your demographics:

AGE RANGE AND LIFE-CYCLE STAGE

Don't say everyone is your target market, or that your property will appeal to people from 9 to 90 years old. Instead, narrow it down to a realistic age range, such as 18 to 34 years old. There are also life-cycle stages, such as the youth market, the parent market, the baby boomer market, etc.

GENDER MIX

What's the ratio of men to women? This is important to sponsors with initiatives targeted to a specific gender. Hair and beauty brands appeal to women, while beer and shaving companies target the male market. Sometimes companies actively want to get more men or women in their consumer base. Since women have been starting businesses at record rates and claiming their economic power, financial institutions actively court the women. Traditional female businesses, like skin care, are expanding to the men's market.

EDUCATIONAL BACKGROUND

Tell the sponsor the percentage of your demographics that have high school degrees, are college educated, and have advanced degrees and certifications. Education may be a key factor in some brands that appeal to people who are more educated or tech-savvy.

BUYING HABITS

What do they buy and why? When are they likely to buy? Sponsors are always pondering these questions, as well as the frequency of purchase and the average size of a purchase. Sponsors also want to know if people are buying for themselves or family members and if they refer the sponsor's product to other people.

INCOME RANGE

Use a median household income range. This is combined income, so it increases if there are two income earners in the house. If there is affluence or your demographics are coming into more economic power, let the sponsor know.

OCCUPATION

Tell your sponsor if your demographic is primarily a certain occupation, such as entrepreneurs, military, sales professionals, attorneys, accountants, etc. Companies target certain professions because they are easy to reach and make good customers. Other sponsors demonstrate category uniqueness by dealing with certain occupations and letting these people know they speak their language.

SOCIO-ECONOMIC STATUS

Is your target audience a group that's emerging as spenders? Displays of consumerism are important to certain parts of the population. New moms discuss educational toys, baby food, and childcare issues. Homeowners recommend paint, windows, lawn care, furniture, and appliance brands to each other.

MARITAL AND FAMILY STATUS

Within your target audience, what's the range of married, single, widowed, and divorced people? How many have children? Parents tell me that they spend all their money on their children and sponsors know this. Just watch a few hours of daytime television and you'll see how sponsors court parents.

DIVERSITY

Definitely mention this because some companies have initiatives in the diversity markets and want to do outreach to minority communities. Multiculturalism and diversity are important concepts in corporate America.

PSYCHOGRAPHICS

Tell the sponsor what motivates your target market and why they buy. What are their fears? What's important to them? Why do they get up in the morning? For instance, the #1 psychographic for entrepreneurs is the desire for freedom and independence.

BUILDING YOUR AUDIENCE

"The aim of marketing is to know and understand your customer so well that the product fits him and sells itself."

— Peter Drucker

LIST-BUILDING WEB SITE

Your web site should collect leads for you and you should know who has visited your site. Most web sites are simply informational, but don't have a way for people to opt in and give their names and contact information. Offer an incentive that people want such as a special report, quiz, book, or training to get them to sign up. Then you can continue to market to these people. The first time people come to your web site, they usually don't purchase. They are looking for information and relationships.

A sign-up box that says "Get Our Newsletter" is not enough anymore. People are inundated with information, so your incentive needs to be something that they find valuable to their lives. Think of the questions people ask you all the time. If you are in the health and wellness field, you can give them a report about the top three super foods for energy, vitality, and brain function. If you advise people about sales and marketing, give them the best marketing strategies for their companies. If you want people to give you their physical address, then offer to ship them a free book or CD audio.

COLLABORATIONS

Power collaborations are the keys to building a great database. Hold joint teleclasses, webinars, live events, and other types of training with people who have bigger lists than you do. This will build your audience quickly. If you want an introduction to a key influencer, ask if you can interview that person for your blog or an article. By using this technique, I added 500 people to my audience in one day.

PUBLIC SPEAKING

Start speaking in public as soon as you can. Don't be afraid! There are great techniques to get rid of the butterflies. I was terrified of public speaking for years and then I found out how much fun and how profitable it is. I went on an amazing trip to Ireland and the best part of the visit was the warmth of the Irish people. It's said that "In Ireland, there are no strangers, just friends you haven't met yet." I always think about this when I do public speaking. I visualize that everyone in the audience is my friend and they really want me to succeed.

When you do public speaking, turn it into a list-building event. Have a giveaway and collect attendees' contact information to win the prize. It could be your book, a training program, a piece of giftware, or a personal care item. If you don't have your own book, buy a book and give it away. Have forms for the attendees to fill out, because some people don't bring business cards.

EVENTS

When you attend events, have a plan about who you want to meet there. Make a follow-up plan that includes setting aside some time the day after the event for follow-up. You can also hire an assistant to do your follow-up and set appointments to talk to your new power players.

Here's a great tip. When you attend an event, find out who books the speakers and make a connection with that person. Tell them about your expertise and your presentation and ask when the next available speaking slot will be. While everyone else is giving their 30-second commercials, you're booking time on the platform to speak to the entire group.

EMAIL MARKETING

Start email marketing as soon as you can and encourage people to forward your email newsletters and articles. Always include an offer in your email marketing. The offer could be to go to your web site and sign up for a something free, watch a video, attend an event, purchase a product, etc.

Authenticity and storytelling sell in email marketing. Show people you're a real person with flaws. Share your mistakes and personal things about your life. Regale people with the obstacles you faced on your success journey. I regularly share stories about my fears, and roadblocks, making it out of the poverty trap, and surviving an abusive relationship. In fact, one of my event attendees told me that my e-zine on fear prompted her to come to my "Sponsor Secrets" seminar, take action, and write a winning sponsor proposal.

SOCIAL MEDIA

You can build a great following quickly on social media. Join groups, write relevant postings, add friends, and do great contests for list-building. This is another chance to show you're a real person. Relate your messages to current news stories and popular culture. When I do postings about my cats, I always get plenty of comments.

VIDEO MARKETING

Make short videos that are consumer-focused and show people who you really are. You can also create videos that show people your lifestyle and unique story. Tell people why you are passionate about your business and how you can help them. Video marketing can also be aspirational. Travel videos are great because they show people what's possible when they become successful. You can decide whether to make your videos professional with quality lighting, editing, captions, background music, and graphics—or do raw videos with a smartphone or handheld device. When you put video on your web site, it increases your opt-ins and list-building.

ONLINE AND MOBILE MARKETING

Publish a blog and post comments on other people's blogs. This is great for SEO (search engine optimization) and more people will find you with Internet searches. You'll also find that people will start subscribing to your blog and some bloggers are very influential in their industry and society.

You can also create your own app for engagement with your brand and include your sponsor in the targeted advertising to your audience. An "app" (or application) is a special software program for a smartphone, mobile device, tablet, or any device that gets you online. One of the best ways to market your app is with third-party endorsements, so ask clients, tech bloggers, and the media to review it. Pay keen attention to any negative reviews and work on fixing any problems.

You can collect people's cell phone numbers for mobile marketing. This is done through SMS (Short Message Service) to cell phones. Mobile marketing is done as permission-based only and you need to give people the opportunity to opt out easily. The open rates for text messages are quite high and this is a great way to build your audience.

SPONSOR BENEFITS

VISIBILITY

When I ask a new client what they have to offer to a sponsor, they usually talk about their visibility benefits. They do so because this is what people are familiar with in the sponsorship world. They go to a sporting event and see sponsor signage around the stadium, or they go to a conference and see banners promoting the event's sponsors. The great thing about visibility benefits is that they are usually low-cost and sometimes even free to you as the sponsee. These are important sponsor benefits, but only part of the value mix in your sponsor proposal.

Hyperlink on your official web site. You can put the sponsors' logos on your "official web site," or include exposure on other web sites you have with a hyperlink to the sponsor's web site. The word "official" is used here because it gives more perceived value. You'll also want to add a sponsor page to your web site with sponsor logos and a three-line description of each sponsor. Some people list all of the sponsors on the home page of their web site and others reserve the valuable home page real estate for their top sponsors. I recommend that, in the beginning, you list all of your sponsors on the home page. After that, where to put the sponsor logos is a choice in your overall sponsor strategy plan.

Signage. If you do an event, you can do on-site signage for your sponsors. This includes banners, tabletops, moveable dynamic signage, video screens, logo apparel, walking characters, videos, rotating slide presentations, etc. If you don't do events, the signage is on your web site, blog, podcasts, email marketing, online documents, web-based training and social media. Most sponsors rank signage as a low-level benefit, but if you don't provide them with signage, they will ask why they don't have any signs. In other words, signage is important, and it can be creative. You can do traditional, as well as innovative, signage where people can interact with the sponsor's brand. One such idea is a portable photo booth.

VIP privileges. VIP privileges include preferred seating, special access, event hosts, meet-and-greets, lounges, receptions, and private time with top talent. Get creative with your VIP experiences, but the minimum you can provide at a live event is preferred seating, their own host, and having meals before everyone else. One of my clients took his VIP guests for a private showing in an art gallery. Another took his VIPs for a tour of the city in a helicopter. Go for "wow" experiences they will share with their colleagues.

Inclusion in social media campaigns. Think of ways to create interactivity for your sponsor with social media. Use contests, videos, discussions, posts and crowdsourcing to involve as many people as possible. For instance, if you're doing a fashion event, you can have people submit their designs for a special prize from your sponsor. Then your fans and followers can vote on who should get the prize. Use social media to engage the audience, encourage sharing, add crowdsourcing (voting on winners) and extend the promotional timeline.

Product placements. Most people think of product placements in television and film, but you can do product placements for your sponsors in other ways. You can incorporate the sponsor's product into your own videos and give it real-person authenticity. Sponsors love video, audio, and written product reviews and testimonials from you and your audience. If you do podcasts or a radio show, put information about your sponsor on the sign-up or information page. Some of my clients do online training (teleclasses and webinars) and thank their sponsors in the opening or the closing. If you let consumers know that your sponsors are making great information and experiences possible, they tend to support those sponsors.

Email marketing. Your email blasts can also promote your sponsors. Add the sponsor logos with click-throughs to the sponsor page of your web site or directly to your sponsor's company web site. You can also do occasional articles about your sponsors. When you send out one-to-one emails, include the sponsor in the signature line.

CONNECTIONS AND ENGAGEMENT

One of the buzzwords in sponsorship is "engagement." It's not enough just to slap a sponsor logo on a web site or a live event. If you want the big bucks, you need to offer a chance for the sponsor to connect with the audience. This leads to return on investment and return on objectives. More connections equal more conversions.

Exhibitor opportunities. At events, give your sponsor an opportunity to set up a vendor table, hand out product information, and talk to prospective customers.

On-site sales. This one seems obvious, but some events are just informational. Let the sponsor know that you encourage on-site sales.

Sampling. A great way for companies to expand their customer base is to offer product samples. This is one of the most honest and powerful forms of advertising. The free sample leads to more orders.

Couponing. For the one-two punch, combine the free sample with a coupon. You've probably seen this at marathons, fundraising walks, and community events. The sponsor gives you, for example, a yogurt sample and a coupon to purchase the yogurt at a retail store. Sponsors love coupons such as these because they can track event- or market-specific results of their advertising and marketing (and sponsorship dollars).

Speaking opportunities. Sponsors love to have their company representatives on the platform. This works for both online and live events. You don't need to give sponsors a full hour to talk to your audience. Perhaps your sponsor rep can introduce you to one of the speakers, or deliver a quick three- to five-minute talk about the company. Maybe the sponsor rep can let people know to enter a contest or come to their booth or web site for more information.

Recognition from the platform. Be sure to recognize your sponsors from the stage or online with lots of gratitude. Let people know that their great experiences would not be possible without the sponsors and encourage your audience to support your sponsor companies.

Gift bag program. If you do a live event, provide gift bags with the sponsors' product samples, marketing information, and their promotional products. You can also print your logo on one side of the official show bag and print your sponsors' logos on the other side.

Contests and giveaways. Contests are great because they are interactive. They can create emotion, desire, and excitement in many unique ways.

Social media are great for contests. You can ask people to send in photos, stories, videos, and testimonials to win the coveted prize. Then you can crowdsource it and have people vote on which of the top finalists should take the spoils of victory.

At your live event, you can do something as simple as a business card raffle or an elaborate contest with voting by the audience. Be sure to photograph the winner with their prize and send it to your sponsor as part of your sponsor report.

Surveys. Sponsors are always looking for research and insights about how to reach their target demographics. Using simple, low-cost tools, you can survey your audience for your sponsors. You need to offer an incentive for respondents who complete the survey, but don't offer them a service or product from your sponsor. This could skew the results. Instead, offer a non-related giveaway or cash prize.

Award presentations. Buy an award and personalize it for your sponsor. I've called this the "Making a Difference Award." Other times sponsors wanted to name the award, so we did a "Community Leader Award." When you present the award to the sponsor, have it professionally photographed and then you can submit it to the media. Sometimes the sponsor will want to show the photos of the award presentation to company employees with an accompanying story. One of my sponsors even put the award in the trophy case at their corporate headquarters.

Product reviews. On behalf of your sponsor, you can write product reviews with articles, email reports, blog posts, create audio video testimonials, etc. Make the product reviews consumer-friendly *and disclose* when your sponsor provides the products.

Cause-related marketing. People want to buy from companies that give back to the community and cause-related marketing is priceless. Cause marketing includes supporting a charity or making the sponsor's brand appeal to a demographic group that needs empowerment. This is also called a "cause overlay" and it's valuable because you'll get more clients, attendees, and sponsors by promoting worthy causes.

Media. For those in the sponsorship and marketing game, the media simply connects buyers and sellers. Think of the media as a collection of different doors people can walk through. It doesn't matter which door, as long as it leads to a sale. Combine traditional and new media in your sponsor proposal.

General press releases. A general press release is what I call "name, rank and serial number." It goes on company letterhead and provides "need-to-know information" about your company, non-profit, event or project. The general press release has a headline, body copy, your web site, photo with captions (not necessary, but nice), and a resource box above the headline that tells *media only* who to contact at the company and how to do it (PR department phone number, PR rep's email address, fax, etc.). Note: This information is not for release to the public and the media respect that request. You can put "For Immediate Release" on the top to let the media source know that they can publish it anytime. If the press release is sent out early, put the suggested publish date on top. Survey results and testimonials give it credibility. Mostly, it needs to be newsworthy. Sponsors are usually mentioned in the bottom paragraph of the general press release.

Dedicated press releases. The dedicated press release has more perceived value because it spotlights your sponsors, even in the headline. It may read, "Brand X Sponsors Amazing Upcoming Event." The dedicated press release will talk about your sponsor and tell the information about your property. Make sure both the dedicated press release and the general press release are keyword-rich to get picked up by more online and offline media sources.

Media buys. You may be able to get some free media by using your media partners and you may be expected to buy traditional and online media. Usually, media buys take place at higher levels of sponsorship, so you can use some of the money the sponsor provides you and buy specific media for them.

Mentions in media interviews. Call or have someone on your team contact as many media outlets as possible to get you interviews. Then mention the sponsor in the media interview only if it's appropriate. This is called "bridging" and it works great in sponsorship campaigns.

Spokesperson's benefits. Did you know you can be a spokesperson for a company? The value of this goodwill for your sponsor is priceless because if people know, like, and trust you, they will be more likely to use products you recommend. A spokesperson's benefits include media, trade shows and events. You can even do a satellite campaign where you do many interviews back-to-back in a short time. The sponsor's public relations department or an outside public relations firm usually coordinates these.

Traditional and online media. Sponsors love traditional as well as new media, so be sure to offer them promotional opportunities that include both. Don't be intimidated by pricing. I've bought inexpensive radio ads that took my sponsor promotion to a new level. When I had a radio station as a media sponsor, they helped me write the script, had one of their most popular on-air hosts read it and added a soundtrack. I'll never forget the time when I was driving and I heard my own radio commercial. I almost had an accident. I got so excited I had to pull the car over to the side of the road.

Naming rights. Naming rights is one of the most valuable incentives you can offer your sponsors. You can give your sponsor naming rights for your entire property or you can create smaller areas your sponsor can own.

Official presenting or title sponsor for your property. Title and presenting sponsor opportunities are valuable because they are promoted in everything you do. Title sponsorship is when the title's brand and yours are married, such as the FedEx Golf Tournament. I recommend presenting sponsorships where your brand is a bit more separated from the sponsor's name. The words "presenting" or "presented by" are in presenting sponsorships. An example is "Stars on Ice Presented by Smuckers." With the presenting sponsorships, it is easier to renew with another sponsor and you can keep your brand identity.

Owned areas. Events like Coachella and South by Southwest have become successful because they provide areas sponsors can "own." These include lounges, pavilions, cocktail receptions, VIP events, meet-and-greets, etc. One of my clients who created a business conference did something brilliant. They took a drab hotel meeting room and turned it into the Verizon Relaxation Lounge. The walls were draped with soft fabric. There were candles and sand sculptures on the tables. Soft music permeated the room and chair massages were offered to reinvigorate the attendees. Even with all this tranquility, there was a video screen displaying the Verizon logo and a booth with Verizon information right outside.

TV commercial campaign. If you have a larger property, your sponsor may help you with a television campaign. They will let you know the features and benefits of their brand and what they want in the creative aspect of the commercial. The campaign can go large and national or stay small and local.

Exclusivity in their category. Sponsorships differ from other types of promotion because the sponsor can pay for exclusivity, which excludes their competitors from your sponsored property. If you have an insurance company, your sponsor may want to be the only insurance brand you promote. Keep your category definitions tight. For instance, when I had Epson, the printer company, as a sponsor, I defined them as a computer printer sponsor, rather than the larger category of communications. Exclusivity usually doesn't hamper your success with sponsors. Most of my clients get one sponsor per category and sometimes you can create a bidding war between two category sponsors that results in a larger sponsor fee. You can make this work to your advantage.

Goodwill of the property. Goodwill is the reason NASCAR gets higher sponsor fees than a small regional car race. This is an intangible, because everyone knows that goodwill is valuable, but it's hard to measure. To build goodwill, start building your audience, media, trust, testimonials, and celebrity status.

Cross-promotions with other sponsors and partners. Sponsors love to do deals with each other, so give them a chance to network. One of the best-kept secrets is that some great collaborations were born out of sponsorship opportunities. Sponsors may see value in your property because they want to get to know influential people on your advisory board. Start making great partnerships and host a sponsor summit, where sponsors can create and nurture relationships.

SPONSOR SUCCESS STORY: SOUTH BY SOUTHWEST
Indie Goes Interactive

South by Southwest (SXSW) is a set of film, music, and interactive festivals and conferences that takes place every year in Austin, Texas. It began in 1987 and, thanks to corporate sponsors, grows every year. The company also runs an educational conference, an environmental event, and a conference focused on innovative startups.

The SXSW Music Festival is the largest of its kind in the world, featuring more than two thousand performers. The festival focuses on up and coming talent. SXSW Interactive focuses on emerging creative technologies.

One of the founders, Roland Swenson, worked at The Austin Chronicle. He tried to persuade the newspaper to do a music festival. The newspaper turned him down, so he decided to do it on his own with the help of co-founder Louis Black, publisher Nick Barbaro, and a booking agent, Louis Meyers.

Since then, South by Southwest has led to singer-songwriter John Mayer signing his first record deal with the Aware label. Films such as the "Hurt Locker" and "Bridesmaids" debuted at SXSW.

The interactive part of South by Southwest was a hit with the tech-savvy attendees and the sponsors. Social media, customized apps, blogs, and mobile marketing became part of the real-time experience.

"Super sponsors" have included Miller Lite, Monster Energy Drinks, Samsung, 3M, Target, American Airlines, Adobe Systems, Esurance, Chevrolet and AT&T.

II. Propose

"You were born to win, but to be a winner, you must plan to win, prepare to win, and expect to win."

— **Zig Ziglar**

Now that you've done your preparation, the next step is to propose what you want to do with your sponsors and why they should open up their checkbook for you. Illustrate how you can add value to their company, what their benefits will be, how you will customize a program for them and how you are dedicated to their success. It all starts with the sponsor proposal.

WHAT'S IN A SPONSOR PROPOSAL?

The sponsor proposal is one of the most important, but least understood, documents in the sponsor game. It's also called the sponsorship deck or prospectus. If you're asking for big bucks, which I highly recommend, then the sponsor decisions are made in the company's teams and committees while you're not even in the room. The sponsor proposal needs to do the heavy lifting and sell for you.

I see many sponsor proposals that are glorified company brochures. It's "all about me, me, me." The best sponsor proposals tell the sponsor about your property and explain how you'll add value to the sponsor.

Write in the third person as if you were a reporter doing a story about your property. Avoid words such as "I, me, my, we, our." Include complete contact information on the footer of each page, including physical address, web site, and phone number.

Do some heavy editing so you can present the right compelling facts. Downsizing is a reality in sponsor companies and many corporate executives are now taking on the jobs of people who are no longer with the company. Their time is extremely limited. Make the sponsor proposal easy to skim, with lots of headings, subheads, and bullets. In fact, a major airline told me that it became a sponsor of mine because they liked the fact that the proposal was written in bullet form rather than paragraphs.

If you submit a sponsor proposal that is not industry-standard, it erodes your credibility. There really is only one chance to create a good first impression. You may not even be able to re-submit to that sponsor because the trust relationship is broken.

The sponsor proposal is the difference between your success and failure. Got it?

COVER PAGE

Your cover page states the name of your property, main sponsor benefit, and contact information. Have great graphics and a professional layout. The most compelling benefit, such as the buying power of your demographic, your credibility, or the strength of your program should be stated here. Remember that the sponsor proposal is about the sponsor, not about you. Therefore, think carefully before you use your company tagline if it doesn't have a compelling benefit to your sponsor. Put some juicy copy that inspires the sponsor to read more.

Include your contact information. You would be surprised how many sponsor proposals I get that don't have any contact information on them. What if a company wants to get in touch with you and give you money? I like every page on the sponsor proposal to have contact information in case the pages become separated.

GOALS FOR SPONSORS

I love to start the sponsor proposal with goals for the sponsors. These are the objectives you have for them, including educating people about their products and services, increasing brand loyalty, awareness, measurable activation, engagement opportunities, growing the customer base, and driving sales. You can customize the goals to the types of companies you're approaching.

DESCRIPTION OF YOUR PROPERTY (EXECUTIVE SUMMARY)

Briefly, tell the sponsor what you do and why they should partner with you. Tell your prospective sponsor how your company is similar to promotions the company has done in the past and how your property is unique. Do your homework and tell the sponsor how your property supports its current initiatives, demographics, goals, and campaigns.

FOUNDER'S STORY

This could be your story or the story of someone you've helped with your business, events, projects, or non-profits. Get real and be vulnerable here. I've never had a company sponsor me. I've had human beings sponsor me because they connected emotionally to my story and my mission. Let your humanity shine and you'll stand out from the other dry, boring sponsor proposals they receive.

STORY OF THE PROPERTY

You may want to continue the story here. Tell the sponsor that because you had an epiphany or a transformational experience, you decided to change your life's work. Let them know more about your property in this section.

SPONSOR BENEFITS

Refer to the section about sponsor benefits and choose the benefits that relate to your property. Tell the sponsor about your assets, multi-benefit packages, and the sponsor opportunities.

DEMOGRAPHICS

Demographics are one of the most valuable assets you have. Unfortunately, this section is most often left out of the proposal. Demographics are also referred to as the target audience or target market. Describe your demographics by using hard data such as age range, gender mix, education, income range, diversity, socio-economics, family status, occupations, life-cycle stage, etc. Remember to include psychographics and buying habits, because these are critical pieces of information for your sponsor.

MEDIA OPPORTUNITIES

List your media partners and media you've been featured in. Explain how sponsors can be part of media campaigns.

MARKETING PLAN

Planning and implementation are most often what separate people who dream from people who achieve. How will people find out about what you do? A marketing plan doesn't need to be a formal, polished document. It just needs to be a description of how you will get the word out and how the sponsor can benefit.

MISSION STATEMENT

The mission statement is part of most business plans and successful businesses get their people to buy into their mission. The mission statement is especially important for causes and charities. It describes your property's ultimate goal and purpose.

ADVISORY BOARD, MANAGEMENT TEAM AND STRATEGIC ALLIANCES

If you know people who are influential in the community, politics, and business, add them to your advisory board. If you are part of a mastermind group, you can put members of the group on your advisory board, including your team. I have a politician on my advisory board and I've never even met her. I knew she was passionate about women's empowerment, so I called her office. Her staff told me to send over a letter of agreement to be on the advisory board and she agreed immediately. Strategic alliances are companies and businesses who can help promote you.

TESTIMONIALS

Let other people sing your praises. Testimonials are powerful, so include full names of the people endorsing you if you can. If confidentiality is important, you can use a pseudonym or abbreviated name. Include the person's photo for more impact and a professional look.

SPONSOR LEVELS AND FEES

This is where you ask for the money. Scary, huh? If you've presented your property well in the body of the sponsor proposal, then the sponsor fee section is the most natural thing in the world. The problem with most sponsor proposals I see is that they are simply a menu of prices without explanations for the sponsor.

CALL TO ACTION

Restate your most compelling benefit and tell the sponsor what you want them to do. They need your guidance here. I prefer to tell the sponsor to call a phone number rather than going to a web site, because the successful sponsorships start with a conversation. Make sure there is someone there to answer your phone professionally. A live person can create rapport and sell better than a web site.

QUICK FACTS SHEET

The quick facts sheet is a snapshot of the most compelling benefits in one or two pages. The quick facts sheet is also called the splash page or the sponsor proposal brief. The first page of the quick facts sheet consists of powerful graphics, title of your property, main benefit, an optional testimonial, and complete contact information.

The second page of the quick facts sheet is the snapshot of your property. I prefer a bulleted list rather than paragraph form for easy skimming. There is no mention of prices or sponsor fees in the quick facts sheet.

Your quick facts sheet is a way to open up a dialogue between you and your prospective sponsor. Sponsors tend to travel and read presentations from sponsor seekers on their smartphones. A two-page quick facts sheet is easier to read on a mobile device than a full sponsor proposal.

HOW TO CREATE VALUE

Here's a great equation to remember in your sponsor offerings:

Value = Reach + Passion + Engagement

You'll want to show your sponsor that you have reach (the number of people exposed to your property or message). Don't worry if you're just starting out. You can build your audience quickly with traditional media, online applications, and collaborations. You have passion for your property, so make sure it shines through when you talk about it with people. I can't believe how many calls I get from prospective clients who describe their property with the same passion they'd use for reading their grocery list. If you're not excited about your property, why should a sponsor be?

Engagement is how the sponsor can interact with an audience, either in person or online. You'll be more successful if you think of ways to provide engagement opportunities for your sponsors.

THINK OUT OF THE BOX

Have brainstorming sessions with your inner circle. If you're a solo entrepreneur, assemble some friends and business colleagues or hire someone to mentor you, and think of some **unique benefits you can offer sponsors. Make your signage** creative. Make your marketing disruptive and think of ways people will share your message. Create videos that go viral. No one remembers the banal. Be outrageous.

I HATE BUSINESS PLANS, BUT I LOVE SPONSOR PROPOSALS

I'm a right-brained creative artist at heart, so I find writing business plans excruciating. However, I love sponsor proposals. Sponsor proposals speak more to my dreams and my vision of changing the world. Sponsor proposals are less focused on financial reports and sales projections. In fact, a sponsor has never asked me about my budget. Sponsors just want to know that you will promote their company, give them return on their investment, and give them a great sponsor experience.

SPONSOR SUCCESS STORY: COMIC-CON
Comic Books Become Big Business

Comic-Con International is an annual event that has filled the San Diego Convention Center with more than 130,000 attendees, making it the fourth most popular comic book convention in the world. Comic-Con has an annual regional economic impact of $162.8 million and is the biggest event in San Diego.

The first convention in 1970 drew only 300 people and was held at a local hotel. It originally highlighted comic books, science fiction/fantasy, film/television, and related popular arts. The convention now includes a larger range of pop culture, such as horror, animation, toys, collectibles, card games, video games, web comics, and fantasy novels.

Hollywood started to take notice. Comic-Con now includes events such as awards ceremonies, the annual masquerade costume contest, and the Comic-Con International Independent Film Festival, which showcases short- and feature-length movies that do not have distribution or distribution deals. There are seminars with comic book professionals, previews of upcoming feature films, and review sessions with top comic book and video game companies. Sponsors have included Warner Brothers, AMC, HBO, Marvel, MTV, Sony Pictures, Showtime, Penguin Publishing, Xbox, SyFy Network and NBC.

PAID, OWNED, AND EARNED MEDIA

Paid media (includes sponsorships): Media buys that can include display ads, commercials, directory listings, paid search, and sponsorships. The challenges are possible clutter with other sponsors and uncertain response rates. The advantages are immediacy and the choice of going large or small scale. The company has complete control over paid media and they are in demand and disruptive.

Owned media: This means media the brand controls, which includes the web site, traditional broadcast, print, blog, podcast, web TV, Internet radio, mobile marketing, and social media. This builds longer-term relationships with existing potential customers. Disadvantages are that there are no guarantees and communication is less trusted. Advantages are control, cost efficiency, longevity, versatility and the ability to connect with niche audiences.

Earned (or free) media: This means favorable publicity gained through promotional efforts other than advertising. Customers become the channel and the message is spread through word of mouth, buzz, and viral online communications. Earned media is often coordinated with owned media and paid media, such as sponsorships. Earned media are often refers specifically to publicity gained through editorial influence. "Earned media" plays a key role in sales. It's transparent and lives on. The media may include any mass media outlets, such as newspaper, television, radio and the Internet. This is the most credible form of media because there is a third-party endorsement.

THINGS IN THE PACKAGE THAT MAY HAVE LITTLE VALUE TO SPONSORS

- Logo on banners, press releases, promotional materials and on-site booth. (*Yeah, so what? Who will see my logo? What other logos will be there? Will there be clutter?*)

- The event will endeavor to publicize sponsor's involvement. (*What does this mean? Who will it be publicized to? What are their buying habits? Where will it be publicized?*)

- Positive public awareness. (*What does this mean, exactly?*)

- Sponsor will get media exposure (*What media? What is the circulation, audience, followers, viewers, and listeners? What are their demographics?*)

SPONSOR PET PEEVES

LARGE ATTACHMENTS

It's thought of as inconsiderate to send your prospective sponsor proposals as large attachments. This means anything over 10MB. Some email programs are not able to open these files or will even bounce back large attachments.

Already, people are a bit skeptical about opening attachments because of computer viruses. The standard format for a sponsor proposal is a PDF (portable document format) document. If you create, or have someone else create, your sponsor proposal in another program, convert it to a PDF. This ensures fidelity when transferred electronically and reduces the file size. If the file is still too large, consult with a professional who can reduce it or make it a click-through link to a web page.

TYPOS

> *"If a word in the dictionary was misspelled, how would we know?"*
>
> **— Steve Wright**

Proofreading is essential. Hire someone to proofread your sponsor proposal and check for grammar and spelling before you submit it to prospective sponsors. I have a panel of sponsors at my Sponsor Secrets Seminar. One of the panelists admitted that when she sees spelling mistakes and bad grammar, she immediately trashes the sponsor proposal. She believes that if the sponsor seeker doesn't care enough to check their own work, then they will be sloppy or lazy in promoting the sponsor's brand.

NOT DOING YOUR HOMEWORK

It's easy to research prospective sponsors by going to their web sites, doing an Internet search, looking at articles, and checking out their social media. The sponsor's time is valuable and they won't waste it with people who should know that their property is not a match from the beginning. For instance, I had a sponsor with a nutritional company at my Sponsor Secrets Seminar. They sponsored health and wellness events. He couldn't believe it when a tobacco company called him looking for sponsorship. Even though you've done your research on the sponsor, ask questions to draw them out when you have your initial conversation. You can demonstrate your knowledge about their company and draw them out at the same time. For example, you can say, "I know that you have initiatives in the small business market. I'd like to know about your upcoming campaigns and how I can help promote you."

LYING

"If you tell the truth, you don't have to remember anything."

— Mark Twain

This forever ruins the credibility of the sponsor seeker. People will say that they've been referred by a key influencer in the company when, in fact, they've never even talked to that person. Here's something egregious a sponsor told me. People would call the sponsor and say they'd talked to the founder of the company–and the founder had been dead for years. Someone will discover such dishonest tactics and you'll surely burn your bridges and never be able to approach the sponsor again.

One of my clients was working out of her home office. She was talking with her sponsor and her baby started crying. The sponsor asked about it and my client had a decision to make. Should she lie or tell the truth? She opted for honesty and said, "I get to work at home and be with my son. Isn't that great?" The sponsor was also a new mom and it gave them something to talk about and a bonding moment. The great thing about the truth is that it's the only story you need to remember.

If someone asks you a question and you don't know the answer, never try to fake it. Instead, admit that you don't know. Then say you'll find the answer and get back to them. This gives you another chance to have a conversation and create honest rapport.

RAMBLERS

Have you ever been on the phone with someone who just won't shut up? Well, imagine being a sponsor with a million things to do, complex decisions to make, and lots of people to manage, every day. Sponsors want you to "bottom-line it" as quickly as possible. They are usually Type-A personalities who don't have time to chat about anything other than your sponsorship and whether it would work for them. Your mission with each conversation is to tell them enough to pique their interest so you can get another meeting and move the process along.

Learning to talk in sound bites will help you with sponsors as well as media appearances. Watch some television interview shows. They are timed to the second and if the guest doesn't get to the point, the interviewer interrupts. Communication is one of the main ingredients of success in business. The best media guests and sponsor seekers are invited back.

LACK OF AUTHENTICITY

When you first contact a sponsor, relate to them as a real person. Show your humanity and even admit to your flaws. Don't sound tired or disinterested. You may even need to get your energy up and walk around with the phone rather than just sit there. If you use positive affirmations and anchoring, then put these techniques into play here.

I encourage you to have telephone scripts, but never sound like you're reading from a script. This is your life's work, so show your passion and commitment. When you have an energetic life force, it becomes contagious and **people want** want to be around you and support you.

WHEN THEY CAN'T UNDERSTAND YOUR PROPERTY

Try your sponsor pitch on a few people. You can even call me and do your sponsor presentation before you contact sponsors. At my Sponsor Secrets Seminar, I've had people who are close to making deals, but the sponsor can't understand what they were trying to sell. Sponsors are busy people and it's not their job to tell you how to do your presentation. This is your job.

Your verbal presentation and sponsor proposal should be clear and benefit-rich to make a great sponsor presentation and get funded.

DOING BUSINESS WITH THEIR COMPETITORS

Buy your sponsor's products. Try out their services and then tell them about your experiences. Let them know that you're referring customers to them. Then you'll have your own story about working with their company. If you want to have sponsors support you, you should support them.

HOW TO CONTACT SPONSORS

PHONE

This is my favorite way to contact the sponsor initially. Sponsorship is a relationship business and you can build a relationship on the phone. Create rapport through conversations, answering questions immediately and assessing your sponsor's mood and personality style by the cadence of their voice. You may need to leave a few voicemails before you talk with the right person, so you'll need a compelling voicemail script. Ideally, you'll reach the person who handles sponsorships, have a few conversations, and then, if possible, move to an in-person meeting.

Be sure to use a good-quality phone line. I talk to lots of people whose cell phones are so bad I can't even understand what they're saying. Or, worse, the call gets dropped in the middle of our conversation. This will annoy the prospective sponsor and they probably won't call you back after a dropped call. Also, make sure any background noise is minimal.

For call-backs, give the sponsor a phone number that's answered by a human, not voicemail. For a professional first impression, don't answer your phone by saying "hello." Always answer the phone with your business name.

IN-PERSON

Meeting with your prospective sponsor in person takes the relationship to the next level. Now you can make eye contact, hand them a hard copy of your sponsor proposal, answer their questions, address their objections, and move ahead to having them open up their checkbook. After the meeting, they feel more connected to you and are more likely to push to fund your property when talking to their teams. They know you're accessible and are more likely to communicate questions. Asking questions is a buying sign, so encourage it!

EMAIL

You may not be able to reach the key influencer by phone or in person, so the next best way is email. Create an email that represents your property and send it to your prospective sponsors with either the full sponsor proposal or the quick facts. If there is interest, the email will progress to a phone conversation and possibly an in-person meeting. Make sure to use a professional email address such as me@mycompany.com.

This shows the sponsor where to access your web site and get more information about your property. The "From" column should either be your name or the name of your company. Make sure the "Subject" line is compelling. Make the email look as personal as possible and avoid "robo-emailing."

ONLINE SUBMISSIONS

Many companies have a form on their web sites that you can fill out and submit for sponsorship. Sometimes these are read and sometimes it's a black hole in space where things go in, but nothing comes back out. If you only fill in the online form, your chances of acceptance are very low and I don't like those odds for you. Sponsors have told me they like it when sponsor seekers respect their process, so do fill out this online form, but don't stop there. Call to find out the next step. Make a note of the date that you filled out the form and any confirmation numbers you get and use your follow-up system.

DIRECT MAIL

You could send a physical letter with a hard copy of the sponsor proposal. This makes a positive impression because now most documents and correspondence are sent electronically. The "lumpy envelope" has a higher open rate, so put in a small gift or promotional product. You could also have an unusual envelope. Contact a direct mail company. They can send your prospective sponsor something that looks like an x-ray or a message in a bottle. Get creative here so you will stand out from the crowd. Also, when you're mailing hard copies of your sponsor proposal, send three or four copies so they can be passed to team members. Remember, teams make many decisions and create a "buzz" in that company.

SOCIAL MEDIA

You can contact sponsors you may not be able to reach by other means of communication through their social media accounts. Find out which social media your sponsors use and send them direct messages, posts, tweets, etc. You can also find prospective sponsors through social media by asking your followers if they know whom to contact in a company on your "Sponsor Wish List." Don't assume sponsors will look at videos you send them. Their time is quite valuable and their working days are full, so they may not have the time to watch videos. Photos and written text work best. If you need to send prospective sponsors a video, let them know about the time commitment. For example, you could ask them to watch a two-minute video about your property. That way, they know it won't be too taxing on their time.

SPONSOR INQUIRY FORM ON YOUR WEB SITE

You can put a page on your web site where companies can inquire about being a sponsor. They can either fill out a form, send an email, or be taken directly to your sponsor proposal. I don't recommend putting your sponsor proposal on the public side of your web site for anyone to see. This is proprietary information and you should only show it to your sponsorship mentors and prospective sponsors. You can set up a special email address such as partners@mycompany.

com or sponsors@mycompany.com. I think the best way to capture the information of prospective sponsors on your web site is to have them fill out a form. Then you can control the information they give you. The more information you ask for, the less likely you'll get inquiries, so I suggest you ask for name, email and an optional phone number. Then send the sponsor your proposal and follow up with next steps.

WHAT DEPARTMENT OF THE COMPANY SHOULD YOU CONTACT FOR SPONSORSHIP?

I've worked with FedEx as a sponsor and everyone asked me who I knew at FedEx. Well, I didn't know anyone. I called and asked for the marketing department. They connected me with the person who could green-light a sponsorship opportunity for me. Because I got the right department and the right person, I worked with FedEx for years.

The marketing department is the best place to start in your outreach to sponsors. I like marketing departments because they have good budgets and they spend most of their time and money promoting their brand. In other words, they get it.

Other departments are corporate communications, public affairs, community relations, corporate or strategic partnerships, communications, brand management, and too many others to list here. If you have a non-profit, you may also want to contact the foundation, corporate giving, social responsibility, or philanthropic arm of the company.

HOW TO TALK TO SPONSORS

LEAD WITH YOUR COMPELLING BENEFITS

Be laser-focused on your top sponsor benefits and just talk about a few compelling opportunities.

Your first conversation is a fact-finding expedition. Listen more than you talk.

Ask the sponsor probing questions and have them reveal their goals, objectives, and visions for the company. Find out about their upcoming campaigns and target demographics. Ask them about past sponsorships, both positive and negative. Then you can go into your presentation and relate it to their goals.

BE BRIEF, BE BRILLIANT, AND BE GONE.

> *"Most conversations are simply monologues delivered in the presence of a witness."*
>
> **— Margaret Millar**

Sponsors don't want to deal with a rambler. Practice presenting your business quickly because the sponsor's time is valuable. Try a few different "elevator speeches" with people in your inner circle. People form their first impressions in a few seconds, so think of the conversation with your sponsor as an audition. Have I made you nervous yet? Here's how to calm your nerves. Breathe deeply before you make the pitch, say an affirmation such as "I'm the best" while rubbing your hands together. This is your physical anchor. Now, if you get nervous when you're talking, you can rub your hands together for a feeling of calmness and confidence.

Lastly, people tend to speak rapidly when they're nervous, which makes people think of the fast-talking car salesperson. Talk a bit more slowly than usual. No one will notice and you'll sound more professional.

MAKE SURE EVERYONE ON THE SPONSOR'S TEAM IS ON THE PHONE CALL

Unless you're asking for a small amount of money, there are usually a few people involved in making the decision to fund you. Companies are now a collection of teams. Try to have all of the people on the team on a conference call so you can tell everyone about your property and answer everyone's questions. You may have a champion in the company who believes in you, but they may need to sell your sponsorship to their bosses and teams.

ALWAYS SCHEDULE A FOLLOW-UP CALL AND MAKE SURE EVERYONE KNOWS THE NEXT STEPS

Sponsorship is a process, so when you're talking to a prospective sponsor, have concrete next steps. Never just say you'll call them back next week.

Set up a date and time to talk. Always use their time zone. If it's hard to pin them down, just say that it's easier to set up a tentative appointment and they can always call you to reschedule if something comes up. This tip has made many lucrative sponsor deals happen for my clients.

Sponsors will give you tests before giving you money, so always do what you say. Your word is your bond. If you can't get the information to the company, let them know you're working on it and haven't forgotten about them. Include the appropriate people, along with the gatekeepers, in the correspondence.

SEND SPONSOR PROPOSALS ELECTRONICALLY AND BY MAIL

It makes a positive impression if you send the proposal both electronically and in hard copy format. If you mail hard copies of the sponsor proposal, send more than one copy so they can pass it to members of their team. Remember, the more buy-in you can get from the team, the more successful you will be with your corporate sponsors.

BE PREPARED WITH A SPONSOR AGREEMENT

Always have an agreement ready, even on your first meeting with the sponsor. They may be willing to sign right away. When they are ready to sign, you may need to fill out tax forms and send them an invoice.

GET SET UP FOR PAYMENTS FROM YOUR SPONSOR

Sometimes it takes them time to set you up in the sponsor's system as a new vendor. Your sponsor fee usually comes in a lump sum rather than payments. That being said, if the sponsor wants to make payments, try for the shortest payment schedule possible.

KEEP EVERYONE IN THE LOOP FOR MORE RENEWALS

When you're getting the initial sponsor fee, you may be dealing with someone at a high level in the company. Then, when the sponsor program starts, someone lower on the corporate food chain will be doing the grunt work, such as getting you the artwork, ad copy, arranging for staffing of exhibitor booths, etc. It's natural to create rapport with the person at the lower level, but keep the key influencer in the loop with everything you're doing.

HAVE TELEPHONE SCRIPTS

You should have a telephone script, especially for your initial contact with prospective sponsors. Don't worry. You won't sound robotic. Even though you've accomplished many things, sponsorship is new to you. It's natural to be a bit nervous. Without a script, you can forget important benefits, or leave a voicemail without your callback information.

ADVISORY BOARD AND STRATEGIC ALLIANCES

> *"It's very important to surround yourself with people you can learn from"*
>
> **— Reba McEntire**

If you want success, you need to hang out with successful people. You can't fly with the eagles if you're down on the ground with the turkeys. Your advisory board and strategic alliances give you great credibility.

When you put your advisory board and strategic alliances on your sponsor proposal, use their photos and a short two-line bio in the advisory board section of the sponsor proposal. When you want people to be on your advisory board, just contact them and let them know that you respect them and their accomplishments. Ask if you can contact them for business advice from time to time. If they support you, they will say yes. Assure them that you won't take up lots of their valuable time or make them attend boring meetings.

ADVISORY BOARD AND MANAGEMENT TEAM

The advisory board is the formal version of the mastermind group. The people in your company are also part of the advisory board and management team. If you're a solo-preneur, don't worry. Invite people who support you and hold your visions in light. If you know people who are influential in business, community and politics, ask them to be on your advisory board. In business, people would rather work with an A-team with a B-idea because they know that the people on the A-team can make things great.

STRATEGIC ALLIANCES

Strategic alliances are companies, not individuals. You may know some business owners or have clients who are glad to help promote you and your property. Place their company logos and describe their businesses in this part of the sponsor proposal.

TESTIMONIALS

These are the rave reviews for you and your property. In the sponsor proposal, you'll place the testimonials with the most compelling parts in bold type with a photo of the person endorsing you. Every time you do work for a client, get a testimonial. There is a magic moment to get a testimonial, which is usually right after you've delivered a finished product or service to a client and they are completely enamored with you. If you don't have testimonials yet, start collecting them.

HOW TO GET TESTIMONIALS

Don't leave it up to people to write their own testimonials. People have the best intentions when they say they'll do this for you, but they get busy and forget. Instead, write a few possible testimonials for them and have them choose their favorite. My favorite tactic is to get a video or audio testimonial. If you're meeting with someone who wants to endorse you, use your phone or video device to film them, or record their audio testimonial. When I'm finished with my sponsor consulting, I get telephone testimonials from my happy clients and record it. You can also get testimonials and endorsements through social media.

CHARITABLE CAUSES AND HOW THEY CAN HELP YOU

"Good causes" have increased exponentially in the past few years and cause-related marketing isn't just hot – it's smoking! This is a sales or promotional partnership between a business and a non-profit for mutual benefit. Money spent on cause-related marketing is a business expense, not a donation, and it's expected to show a return on investment.

There is something called the "halo effect" where, if a company gives back to the community, people perceive the company as a good corporate citizen and consumers feel better about buying from that business. A classic example is that Target stores give a portion of their proceeds to help causes such as feeding hungry families and helping local schools. People feel better about buying for their children and families from Target because they are a socially responsible company.

If you are a charity, this is one of the juiciest benefits for your corporate sponsors and it's why the best non-profits such as Susan G. Komen for the Cure, Habitat for Humanity, St. Jude's Hospital, and Make a Wish have been so successful.

With a cause overlay, your property will reap positive publicity from the non-profit, receive additional marketing support from your sponsor and add a valuable benefit that could be the difference in attracting or retaining sponsors.

You may be **wondering** how you can give to a cause if you're just starting out. Many large companies only give 1.5 percent of their net profits to their chosen charity. Knowing that, you can start small and then increase your charitable donations as you grow. You can also donate needed supplies or help with fundraising.

This is another benefit to having a charitable partner. If you're working with an established charity, they have followers, so they can promote you. They can have you speak at their events. Many of the biggest movers and shakers sit on charitable boards and this is how you can also meet future clients and sponsors.

SHOULD YOU START YOUR OWN NON-PROFIT?

Many of my clients ask me if they should start their own charity rather than partner with an established non-profit. You get more control this way and I've seen it work successfully.

It's a personal decision. You'll need to do an honest assessment on whether you have the time to set up and run another business. Even though this is a charity, it still operates under the same rules of business. Otherwise, it will not succeed. One of my pet peeves about charities is "poverty mentality." People think they don't need to spend money to run their charity. Sometimes they operate by **different rules**, let egos take over, and don't pay attention to marketing and promotion. Just look at successful charities and you'll see that they are capitalists at heart. The more money you make, the more people you can help.

If you start your own charity, make sure it's a 501c3 non-profit because this is what sponsors prefer. Sometimes sponsors may want to support a charity for the tax benefits and you can get money from foundations. You'll need to be patient with all the paperwork that's needed to start your own charity. Your accounting needs to be pristine, so consult an attorney and accountant at the beginning so you can set up everything correctly.

> **SPONSOR SUCCESS STORY: FIRST BOOK**
> Magic of Reading for Children
>
> Remember your first book? First Book does and they want to create the memory and magic of the first book for a child. They concentrate on low-income areas where children have limited access to books in their homes and classrooms.
>
> They've distributed more than 100 million books in the last 20 years and studies show that interest in reading more than triples among children who received books from First Book. According to Kyle Zimmer, president of First Book, "We're focused on impact: We leverage the work of heroic teachers, give volunteers the tools they need, and help raise reading scores. Recently, a principal reported that First Book allowed her teachers and volunteers to elevate quality, create a culture of reading, and increase Academic Performance Index scores by 107 points. This is change we are delivering."
>
> Some of First Book's sponsors have included KPMG, Ruth's Chris Steak House, Macy's, Cheerios, and Target.

MEDIA SPONSORS

Media sponsors help you get the word out. Media is usually in-kind, and there is tremendous value in trade sponsors such as media. I got a $25,000 radio promotion campaign without a dime coming out of my pocket. Media sponsors can be yours for low cost or even no cost. You can do amazing publicity and grow your business, event, non-profit or project through the support of the media.

Here's how it works. Send the media the same sponsor proposal you've prepared for your cash and corporate sponsors. When you contact the media, ask for different titles. In broadcast media, you might ask for the general manager or promotions department. You may also talk with a separate public relations firm or media buying service for your prospective sponsor. Even though media is in-kind, don't mention in-kind on your sponsor proposal. Instead, you can say, "We'll trade our $25,000 package for your $25,000 package."

Then work out what you'll trade your media partner in the sponsorship. You can offer visibility, such as an exhibitor opportunity, distributing their marketing materials, contests, speaking opportunities, etc. Traditional media oulets love to get out into the community, so give them opportunities to connect with their core consumers. Also, include online media in your mix, which includes blogs, podcasts, web sites, social media, etc.

You'll want to get as much media as possible, so there is no exclusivity with your media sponsors. They don't expect to be exclusive.

If you're a for-profit business, then your charitable partner will be invaluable here. If you're a non-profit, great! Certain media, such as broadcast (radio and television), need featureworthy causes and public affairs programming to keep their licenses. Play up the charity and it will open many media doors for you. I'm in one of the most competitive media markets in the country, Los Angeles. It's hard to break in here, but I got on some monster radio stations because of my charitable partner, Junior Achievement. We brought in the students who won awards for the businesses they created. They were so excited to be interviewed on live radio. The non-profit got great exposure and, by the way, they mentioned my event, the Women's Small Business Expo. Everyone was a winner.

SPONSOR STRATEGY:
GET YOUR MEDIA SPONSORS FIRST

If you want to build your audience, you can get your media sponsors first and then leverage them to get cash sponsors. If your database is small, you might add 30,000 people with just one media sponsor. This is called extended reach and it's valuable to your corporate sponsors. Go for traditional as well as online media in your marketing plan. One of my clients got 30 percent of the attendees at his event from the local newspaper.

WHAT'S THE DIFFERENCE BETWEEN MEDIA SPONSORS AND MEDIA APPEARANCES?

Media sponsors have a relationship with you. A media appearance is a one-time exposure opportunity. You don't have a promotional agreement in place if it's a one-time media appearance, but you can contact your media sponsors and talk to them. You agree to promote your media partners and they agree to promote you.

III. Promote

"If you're not a risk taker, you should get the hell out of business."

— Ray Kroc, McDonald's Founder

You've done the preparation, created your sponsor proposal, and secured your sponsor deal. Congratulations and well done. Now it's time to celebrate.

It's time to start promoting your sponsor to secure your long-term connections, multi-year contracts and renewals. You need to protect your rights in the sponsor deal, so have your sponsor sign an agreement. This helps to create a great relationship because everyone's role is clear from the beginning.

You'll need some content and creative from your sponsor and its accounting department will have you sign some forms.

You would be surprised at the number of people who get a check from their sponsor and then don't talk to them again until they want more money. When there was no communication, what do you suppose the sponsor is thinking? They want to know what you did for them during the contract period and how you added value to their company before they open up their checkbook again.

You'll want to document everything you do to promote your sponsor, and give your sponsor regular reports. Communication is the key here and it can make getting sponsor renewals as easy as sending them a new invoice.

GET CONTENT FROM YOUR SPONSORS

Now that you have your sponsor deal, you'll need some things from your sponsor. Some of my clients use a checklist of what they need from their sponsors, which includes deadlines. Sponsors get busy and sometimes they need a reminder to send things on time. My sponsors have made me wait until the press deadline before they gave me the ads for the program book. Start your requests early and keep notes of when you received your content and who sent it to you.

Some companies are protective of their brands and want approvals on everything you use to promote them. Others are more relaxed about their branding. The culture of each company is different.

GRAPHICS

Have the sponsor send you their creative content, including logos, image files, photos, ads, product shots, anything they want you to use to promote their company. You may be able to get these from the sponsor's web site, but ask for their approval before you use anything you've obtained from the sponsor's web site. Logos and graphics go through transitions, so you need to be sure that the visual branding is current.

VIDEOS

Sometimes you can find sponsor videos online and other times, they need to send you the videos or video links. If you create your own videos or user-generated videos from your audience, make sure the sponsor approves it before it goes live.

COPY

Have the sponsor send you marketing copy and blurbs about the company and its products and features. You can also get company descriptions from the sponsor's web site. Then you can do lots of creative copy for the sponsor, including blog posts, articles, product reviews, social media, traditional advertising, direct mail, online campaigns, press releases, sales pages, and marketing materials.

SURVEYS

If the sponsor wants you to do a survey for them, they may use a certain survey web site so they can calculate the results. You can also use any of the myriad survey tools and web sites on the Internet to poll your audience about the sponsor and the brand. The sponsor may also want to provide an incentive to encourage people to answer the survey. You'll get the highest survey response at live events. If you're doing an evaluation at your live event, ask the sponsor which questions they would like you to ask your audience.

COMPANY REPRESENTATIVES

Get complete contact information, correct spelling of the names, job titles and roles of everyone on the sponsor's team. Know which people to copy in your correspondence and who is in charge of what aspects of your sponsor program including how you'll get paid.

OTHER INFORMATION

If you're providing a branded area for your sponsor at your live event, they might want to know the size so they can design an interactive display. Contests need a concept, timeline, voting information, and announcement of prize winners.

PHOTOGRAPH AND DOCUMENT EVERYTHING

Take your still and video camera to every event or special meeting. If you can, hire a professional photographer and videographer. Then you can send photos and videos to the sponsor during your contract period and put them in your sponsor reports. Still photos are preferable because sponsors are less likely to click through and watch a video. Instead, put a still from the video in your sponsor report. A picture really is worth a thousand words.

SEAL THE DEAL AND GET THE RENEWALS

SPONSOR AGREEMENT

Make it brief and call it an "agreement," not a contract. The word "contract" has a negative connotation with people.

Also, don't ask them to "sign" it. They might think they're signing their life away. Instead, ask them to authorize it or, if you have a good relationship, ask them to autograph it. My company has a great, non-threatening, one-page sponsor agreement, so feel free to contact me if you'd like some information.

SPONSOR REPORTS

I've seen some sponsorship reports that are beautiful bound books and some reports that are only one page. It's up to you how elaborate you want to make your sponsor reports. I recommend that you do them at least once a quarter. Don't just send the sponsor the report. Set up a phone call or live meeting with your sponsor to go over the report and explain how you've added value to their company with your sponsor program.

In addition, ask the sponsor for honest feedback and be willing to hear it. This could be the difference between success and failure. When one of my bank sponsors had a criticism about my program, I was devastated, but I fixed the issue and it became a multi-year contract. They sponsored me for five more years.

RENEWALS

Renewals and multi-year contracts are some of the coolest aspects of corporate sponsorship. You get the money for a specific contract period. I recommend one year. Then you can get a renewal for the next year. The best way to get renewals is to keep the lines of communication open with your sponsor throughout the year. If you mention them, send them an email, or give them a quick call to let them know. If they show up at your event, take plenty of photos of them and send the pictures to your sponsor. Subscribe to their blogs, email marketing, and social media, and put up posts and comments. Keep abreast of their current advertising and media and praise them on their campaigns.

I did a radio interview and mentioned one of my airline sponsors. When I got back from the radio studio, I sent off a quick email to my sponsor, saying I'd talked about them on the air. They sent me back a glowing thank-you. This kind of informal communication helps build rapport and renewals.

SUPPORT YOUR SPONSORS

> *"Let us be grateful to people who make us happy; they are the charming gardeners who make our souls blossom."*
>
> **—Marcel Proust**

Sponsors have told me off the record that part of the reason they don't renew with properties is that the property didn't support them. This is tragic, because supporting your sponsor is inexpensive and necessary for success.

When Microsoft was my sponsor, I bought Microsoft Office products for my team and myself. When I worked with Dun & Bradstreet Credibility Corporation, I bought their Credit Builder product for my own business.

If you have a bank sponsor, open an account at that bank. It doesn't need to be your main account, but you need to experience the bank's resources and relationships. Then you'll have an authentic story you can tell your audience about the sponsor. Why would other people support the sponsor if you don't even support them?

People ask me what it costs to support the sponsor. I say it doesn't matter. It's usually not that expensive. Sometimes they even send you product samples as part of your sponsor deal. Supporting your sponsor creates a better relationship with them and your audience. It also makes you more successful with your sponsor renewals.

SPONSOR SUCCESS STORY: ALEX'S LEMONADE STAND

Even a child can get sponsors

Patrick Edwards' fight against cancer began early in his life. Patrick's birth and babyhood seemed normal, but toward the end of his first year, his mother felt sure something was not right. Up one night with him at 3:00 am, his mother noticed a lump in his belly. Patrick was diagnosed with Wilms' Tumor, a rare type of children's cancer. His mom said, "I didn't even know what the word 'oncologist' meant at the time of his diagnosis." Patrick's family received help from Alex Scott, a little girl they'd never met.

Alex Scott was only four years old and suffering from cancer. Her young life consisted of going to the hospital for continual treatments. She announced to her parents that she wanted to start a lemonade stand in the front yard to fund cancer research at "her hospital." The media and sponsors found out about what she was doing and, by the time this brave little girl passed away at eight years old, she had raised more than $1 million for cancer research. Volvo became a sponsor and had Alex's Lemonade Stand events in its dealerships, where individuals, schools, and businesses could donate to cancer research. Then Applebee's, Old Navy, Rita's, Country Time Lemonade, and Northwestern Mutual became corporate sponsors.

Now the foundation has raised more than $80 million toward fulfilling Alex's dream of finding a cure for childhood cancer and helping kids like Patrick Edwards. Alex's Lemonade Stand has helped countless children and has funded more than 450 research projects nationally. There are Alex's Lemonade Stand events all over the country, as well as The Lemonade Run, the Lemon Ball, culinary events, and a camp for kids.

Patrick Edwards' mom found the Alex's Lemonade Stand Foundation when she was looking for ways to fight back against childhood cancer. She wrote, "Alex's Lemonade Stand Foundation gives me a way to feel some sort of control in the fight against childhood cancer, when really... I am powerless against it all. It allows me to fight, in whatever small way I can, instead of sitting back and waiting for others to do something." After their first lemonade stand event, they did many more and continued Alex's legacy of raising money for childhood cancer.

"My hopes and dreams for Patrick are the same as any mother, yet are amplified due to his cancer diagnosis. I hope for a bright, healthy future for him. I dream that he will succeed in life and will grow to be a man with a loving family of his own. I pray he will fight for what he believes in and stand up for those who need a voice. I pray he continues to be kind and gentle and brave... and cancer free!"

Alex Scott's story illustrates that with sponsors, you can create your legacy, transform lives, and change the world. Alex was a hero and now is the time for you to step up and be a hero. If a child can do it, so can you.

STEPS FOR GETTING YOUR SPONSORS

Here are the steps for getting your corporate sponsors:

1. Create your Sponsor Wish List. Remember to put down top-tier and second-tier sponsors and go beyond your love marks, the brands that you use and recommend.

2. Get sponsor-ready. Develop the image of your property and make it desirable to corporate sponsors. Update your visual branding and marketing materials.

3. Create your sponsor action plan. Write down your dreams and describe how you want to achieve them. Decide if you want to do your own sponsor strategy or hire a company to help you.

4. Create your sponsor proposal to attract your corporate sponsors. Write your sponsor proposal and quick facts sheet or have someone else create it with professional graphics, layout, and words that sell. Don't be afraid to ask for the big bucks.

5. Contact your sponsors. Call, email, and contact your prospective sponsors online. Be sure to have a captivating sponsor pitch letter and telephone scripts for talking with a company representative and leaving a compelling voicemail that will be returned.

6. Negotiate the sponsor deals. Agree on the sponsor fees and sign an agreement. Go through the company process of filling out paperwork, asking for creative, and finding out what kind of language the sponsor wants to use to describe its brand.

7. Continue to fund your dreams. Create quarterly sponsor reports and communicate with sponsors to let them know how you are promoting their company. Then wash, rinse, and repeat. It's time to get the renewals and keep on doing what you love.

WHAT ACTIONS WILL YOU TAKE?

Now you've learned how to get started with corporate sponsorships. This book is just the start of your incredible journey. It's time to take action. Don't implement the strategies by yourself. Create your sponsor action plan. Then create your sponsor team. You can hire someone to mentor you, create the proposal, and contact the sponsors for you. The most important thing is to implement what you've learned.

One of the questions I'm most asked in media interviews is: What is the difference between successful people and people who just dream of success? It comes down to one word: Action. We've been taught that knowledge is power, but that's only half of the story. Taking *action* on that knowledge is where your true power lies.

MAKE YOUR BIG DREAMS HAPPEN

"When I'm old and dying, I plan to look back on my life and say 'wow, that was an adventure,' not 'wow, I sure felt safe.'"

—Tom Preston, Co-Founder, Werner Github

We've been inspired to have big dreams, but those dreams need funding. The problem is, we don't know how to get the resources to bring our dreams to life.

Create a mission statement for your life. My mission is to live well, have fun, and help other people achieve their greatness. I've turned down clients who were obnoxious because working with them wouldn't be any fun—and life is just too short. Now I only work with people I like and respect. Helping people achieve their greatness is the most rewarding part of my life.

I've gone from being a victim to being the master of my own life. It's important for me to live well. When you don't have the tyranny of struggling to pay your bills, you can truly change the world.

There's nothing like the euphoria you'll feel when you land your first sponsor deal. This is the culmination of all your hard work and the start of the path to your dreams. The sponsor relationship is the ultimate mastermind and you'll create powerful partnerships. Come into sponsorship with the wide-eyed innocence of a child and be open to learning about how to improve and skyrocket your business. Be a sponge. You'll get to peek behind the curtain and see how some of the most successful companies in America operate. The only constant in business is change, so always look for ways you can evolve as a business and grow as a person.

The most phenomenal people I've met have been the people in the sponsor departments. They fund worthy businesses, events, projects, and non-profits. They are wonderful people. Estée Lauder, the cosmetics queen, said that everyone has an invisible sign on his or her forehead that says, "Make me feel important." Show sponsors your gratitude by sending them thank-you notes, e-greetings, and gifts. A little bit of kindness will reap big rewards.

GO FOR IT

America's top companies use the power of corporate sponsors. Why not you? Why not now? By knowing what sponsors want, you'll get the confidence to hold your head high and know that you have great value and benefits to offer your corporate sponsors.

You are not alone. Even when I was working from my kitchen table, I knew I didn't need to do it by myself. I found a company that had experience with corporate sponsorship and asked them for their help in writing my proposal and approaching sponsors. I surrounded myself with incredible people who could mentor me. I wasn't alone and you don't need to be either. Please feel free to contact me if you have any questions. I'm always glad to help you.

Sponsors give you the resources to help more people, live your passionate life, and do it bravely. You can create your legacy and transform people's lives. Your spirit has been sparked and I wish you all the success in the world.

Now go out and step into your greatness. I'll be waiting to hear your success story…

Author's Note

I would love to hear from you.

I hope you were elevated and inspired by this book. I've dedicated it to the winning spirit of people just like you.

If you have any questions, thoughts, insights, breakthroughs, or stories you would like to share, please email me at Linda@SponsorConcierge.com. You can also call 310-337-1430, or write to me at Sponsor Concierge, P.O. Box 83639, Los Angeles, CA 90083. Please note that any stories submitted may be used for future publication. Individual stories may or may not be acknowledged. However, as in this book, names and other details may be camouflaged to protect your privacy.

Being able to inspire people like you means the world to me and I wish you the best of success with your sponsorships. Live well, have fun, do what you love, change lives, and share your gifts with the world!

To your success,

Linda Hollander
310-337-1430
Linda@SponsorConcierge.com